CREATING A
TECH
SABBATH
HABIT

CREATING A
TECH SABBATH HABIT

Unplug your Mind, Restore your Spirit, & Transform your Technology Lifestyle

BRYAN BROOKS

TATE PUBLISHING & Enterprises

Published by Tate Publishing & Enterprises, LLC
127 E. Trade Center Terrace | Mustang, Oklahoma 73064 USA
1.888.361.9473 | www.tatepublishing.com

Tate Publishing is committed to excellence in the publishing industry. The company reflects the philosophy established by the founders, based on Psalm 68:11,
"The Lord gave the word and great was the company of those who published it."

Book design copyright © 2011 by Tate Publishing, LLC. All rights reserved.
Cover design by Kristen Verser
Interior design by Christina Hicks

Published in the United States of America
ISBN: 978-1-61777-404-1
1. Religion / Christian Life / Personal Growth
2. Body, Mind & Spirit / General
11.04.05

Dedication

To my amazing and beautiful wife, Karyn, and my two perfectly and wonderfully made kids, Shawn and Danielle, who stuck it out with me while I learned some difficult lessons. Thank you so much for giving me grace when I didn't deserve it and your abundance of unconditional love. I love you guys with all my heart and soul.

To my church family, close friends, relatives, and business associates who in some way got affected by my out of control technology lifestyle and habits, I sincerely apologize.

Acknowledgements

First and foremost to my Lord and Savior Jesus Christ for His continued grace and mercy toward me. You gave me the revelation for this book and sent me on the pursuit of an unplugging journey, which I so desperately needed. You also provided me with the inspiration, motivation, passion, and courage to share details of my personal testimony with the world through the writing of this book and without which I am nothing.

To my amazing godly wife, Karyn Brooks, who has not only walked with me through the most dismal moments of my unplugging journey, but without your prayers, continuous encouragement, and unconditional love and grace for me, this book, as well as my marriage of eighteen years, would not have been possible.

To my children, Shawn and Danielle Brooks, who have given to me more than they have received. Your undying love, patience for me, and continual measures of grace touch my heart in ways only a father can truly know.

To Jeanie Jacobsen, my spiritual mom and mentor, thank you for helping me better understand God's priority model for my life.

To my senior pastors at The Father's House, Dave and Donna Patterson, whose wisdom, love, and generous spirits have touched me and changed me from the inside out. Thank you so much for giving me fresh practical perspective from God's Word and showing me what it looks like to be a true Christ-follower and to run after Jesus with all my heart.

To my executive pastor at The Father's House, Mark Sligar, what an amazing man of God you are. Your great sense of humor, wisdom, generosity, and spiritual counsel I sincerely appreciate. I value our friendship.

To my worship pastors at The Father's House, Joseph and Tosha Zwanziger, your music is a constant infusion to my soul and always lifts my spirits and blesses me. I deeply value our friendship.

To my dear mom, Charlene Brooks, for bringing me into this world and making me the man I am.

To my publishing company, Tate Publishing, thank you for your hard work, ideas, patience, and creative ways that you have taken the content, design, and distribution of this book and made it come alive.

And finally, to all my readers, thanks so much for your willingness to be open-minded to trying something new. As a new author, you never know or have any idea how a book will impact people's lives. I pray that this book impacts your life as much as it has mine and that technology never becomes a curse to you, only a blessing, that it truly does enhance your life.

Table of Contents

Preface

While there is no question that technology serves many worthwhile purposes in our everyday lives, having the self-control to not allow it to overwhelm our lives and take a break from it is much easier said than done. Ongoing studies continue to expose people's technology lifestyle habits, which confirm the increasing dependency and overwhelming impact it has on our daily lives and those around us—things like crippling our attention spans, stealing our rest, isolating us from our precious relationships, and damaging the intimacy of face-to-face conversations with those we love.

If you told me over a decade and a half ago that technology had the ability to rule and overwhelm my life, I would have never ever believed it. That's because the technology available during the late eighties and early nineties was quite a bit different than it is today, and a lot less of it was available. But in today's technology-driven, constantly connected world, the cold, hard reality is that you can easily find yourself quickly headed for an overwhelmed life if you are not careful in the way you manage it.

As a result of allowing too much technology to enter and rule my life for more than ten years and never making time to take a break from it, moment by moment, time after time, important parts of my life disintegrated in front of my very eyes. Many missed opportunities to spend time with my kids, special moments I had set apart and planned but turned down with my wife, neglecting my friendships and continually sacrificing growing my relationship with God, all to pursue spending time with technology.

The writing of this book, *Creating a Tech Sabbath Habit*, is truly a life message for my family and me, I say it is a life message because to me it was more than just the writing of this book—it was a journey of personal change, reflection, and a lifestyle transformation. The journey in its entirety has literally restored my life from the inside out in many ways, and now I am enjoying life more than I ever had. Learning how to regularly unplug myself, set boundaries, transform my behaviors around the way technology is implemented in my life, slowing down and rediscovering God's Sabbath, His command of rest, restoration, and rejuvenation has truly awakened my spirit and stirred my soul in new ways that I could have never personally imagined.

After many years of allowing technology to drive my every waking moment, it was in August of 2008 that God finally got through to me. It was like He hit me over the head with a spiritual two-by-four and woke me up. It was through this awakening process—combined with my own personal life-changing technology-unplugging journey—that God led me to pursuit over the course of a year that this book was birthed and my life transformation began.

Now living out my tech Sabbath habit plan, I am proud to say that technology no longer rules or overwhelms my life but rather enhances it in a positive way. As a result, I live a more God-focused, balanced technology lifestyle, and I am proud to say that I do spend a lot less time with technology and more time on the important aspects of my life (family, friends, growing in my relationship with God).

Bryan Brooks

Introduction

Technology is powerful, amazingly incredible, and has become an integral part of the fabric of our daily lives. It enhances our lives in many ways. It has proven to allow us to do many astonishing things once thought nearly impossible. It has made our lives function more proficiently and efficiently, as well as provided us with even more creative ways to occupy our time. Here are a few examples: a personal GPS unit that has a guided voice which provides precise turn-by-turn directions when we travel to unfamiliar places, a laptop that provides us the ability to work remotely from the comfort of our homes, or how about a smart phone that provides us the capability to send a text, picture, or video message or make a quick phone call to a family member at home when we are at the grocery store and can't remember the right brand of milk, soda, or coffee so we don't have to run back home and check for ourselves. Or lastly, the Internet, which gives us instantaneous access to news and information and connects us via live video/audio to friends and family in other states or even on the other side of the world within seconds.

Technology has a lot of benefit to our lives. But with all of the technology advancements this world has seen over the years that are available to us today, it makes me wonder how many people are actually receiving the benefits of it and how it really is enhancing our lives. For example, family time in 2008 dropped by more than 30 percent per month to 17.9 hours as a result of the Internet.[1] Forty-eight percent of Americans feel their lives have become more stressful in the past five years as a result of technology.[2] More than half (58 percent) say technology has led people to spend less time with their families and friends.[3]

Graduating from technical college in October 1990, I felt a sense of accomplishment and achievement. For the first time in my life, I was ready to tackle the world, enter the workforce, and start learning about the amazing world of technology. As a direct result of technology still being in its infancy in 1990, there was little of it in my life, and I would say that overall it was definitely enhancing. But over the years, after I got married and started a family, I continued to acquire more technology and adapted my lifestyle around it. Without realizing it, I soon allowed a dangerous transition to take place—the transition of technology as a tool that enhanced my life to a leash that overwhelmed it.

It was August 2008 when technology officially overwhelmed me and took over my life. My weeks and weekends were tied up with some sort of technology interaction. My laptop became more important than spending time with my wife and kids, my smart phone would end up sleeping next to me in my bedroom, TV watching took priority over spending time with my friends, I was wasting more time on the Internet than reading my Bible and spending time with God. The list goes on and on. Technology became the new god in my life, and I was tied to it. I could not see how, if I were to unplug or get rid of some of it, I would be able to function. Apparently, though, I am not alone. More and more people are struggling with this same problem and issue. Allowing technology to enter and rule one's life and not getting a break from it seems to be becoming more commonplace. Jesus said in Matthew 6:24 (NIV): "No one can serve two masters for either he will hate the one and love the other, or else he will be loyal to the one and despise the other." Do you serve the god of technology? Hopefully not. For me, unfortunately, my master became technology, and there was no doubt that I was its slave. I got so wrapped up in it that it ended up taking top priority in my life for many years.

Bryan Brooks

As evidence that technology is entering, ruling, and impacting people's lives in a negative way, consider just a few of these shocking statistics: Broadband users spend an average of 48 percent, which is almost half of their free time, online in a typical weekday.[4] In 2008, adults and teens in the US spent nearly five months (3,518 hours) watching television, surfing the Internet, reading daily online newspapers, and listening to personal music devices[5], and 65 percent of US consumers are spending more time with their computers than with their significant others[6]. These not-so-encouraging stats provide strong evidence that people are allowing a dangerous transition to occur. It is the transition from enhancing to overwhelming. It is real and is taking place in peoples lives every day.

How is technology affecting your lifestyle currently? Would you say it's enhancing it or overwhelming it? For a lot of us, this is not an easy question to answer, unless you use little or no technology in your life. Many of us become victims of what I refer to as the LG (Latest and Greatest) syndrome; we feel a sense of obligation to it, it creates undue stress on us, we feel helpless and lost without it, it affects our relationships, we feel out of touch and disconnected from the world when we are not using it, and when it doesn't do what we expect, we get frustrated.

"Fifty-two percent of Americans describe their most recent experience with a computer as one of anger, sadness, or alienation."[7] Seventy-six percent of adults admit to being frustrated by technology.[8] The most disturbing fact is that people continue to sacrifice things that should not be sacrificed, like our relationship with God, our families, and friends to spend time with metal and plastic. Thirty-five percent of smart phone users would choose their smart phones over their significant others if they were to choose one to live without.[9]

More often than not, we buy the technology, embed it into our daily lives without thinking about the ramifications, and then later on down the road, we end up paying some devastating consequences. If you use technology of any kind over along period of time without detaching yourself from it on a frequent basis, you are destined for an overwhelming leashed life—one where technology drives and defines everything you do—and if you live your life this way, there is no doubt that at some point you will become a slave to it. Remember this: Any technology that becomes part of your lifestyle should serve the purpose of enhancing it...not overwhelming it.

Prologue

It was Friday, August 22, 2008, when I was working nose to the grindstone upstairs in my home office on a work project for a client that was under a tight timeline. I worked on the project throughout my week and put in several long, taxing days. Deep in mental exhaustion and under major stress, I knew I needed to push myself to finish and meet the project deadline so I did not have to worry about working over the weekend. On this particular day, I worked for more than fourteen hours straight, with only one ten-minute break.

For some odd reason, it seemed to be a major challenge to concentrate on this particular day; the interruptions and disruptions just wouldn't stop. I was also having a ton of weird technology issues. The day started off with my smart phone constantly going off between phone calls, calendar reminders, voice mails, and e-mails. Then because of my lack of eating all day, my stomach was empty and constantly grumbling with hunger pains. My eyes were blistering red, dry, and irritated from computer screen strain. I had a pounding headache from lack of sleep the night before because I spent multiple hours working late into the night. My back was sore from the improper sitting position that I was in all day long. And to top things off, my printer kept saying it was offline, then it was low on ink, the paper kept jamming, and my laptop was locking up. Applications were randomly shutting down, and my Internet connection speed was being painfully slow. Needless to say, my frustration level was building rapidly.

On top of all that, my wife was trying to talk to me about important family matters since earlier in the day, which I was ignoring her about. She wasn't happy at all, and actually she was quite irritated and giving me the "I am really not happy with you" look. I also previously promised my kids earlier in the week that we would go to the movies on Friday night. It was already 7:00 p.m., and I was nowhere near completing the work I needed to finish. As it ended up, I broke yet another promise to my kids. Wow. What a perfect recipe for disaster, eh?

Well, after some serious convincing from my wife, she was able to get me to step away and take a break from things for a few minutes. As I begrudgingly stepped away, mumbling my frustrations under my breath to get something to drink and eat, I heard this small voice say, *Bryan, you need to take a tech Sabbath; your habits and priorities are out of control.* As I was processing what I thought I heard, I then heard two scriptures: "For where your treasure is, there your heart will be also" (Matthew 6:21, NIV) and "The Sabbath was made for man, not man for the Sabbath" (Mark 2:27, NIV).

Filled with guilt, condemnation, and conviction, I proceeded to try to push aside what I heard and sat back down in front of my computer to finish getting my work done. For some weird reason, though, after I sat back down, I could not stop thinking about those two scriptures and the words I heard. As a matter of fact, I stopped, leaned back in my chair, and quietly asked myself, "God, is that you?" and "God, if that is you, can you please help me understand what you are trying to explain to me?"

God's message was quite clear. He revealed to me in that moment what I had done to myself for over a decade and a half. I finally reached the point where technology took over my life. Stressed, frustrated, tired, and overwhelmed by the work I so desperately needed to get done, coupled with the continuous exposure of technology in my work and my personal life, I hit a wall in more ways than I could have possibly imagined. God, in an obvious way, pointed out to me that I needed to set down the god of technology, take back my life, and get some rest. It's like God hit me with a spiritual two-by-four and woke me up. The lack of established boundaries, the never-ending workday, and the LG (latest and greatest) syndrome contributed to a massively tall pile of bricks that were silently wavering for many years and waiting for the right opportunity to come violently tumbling down on me. Technology had been overwhelming me for a while. My wife and kids knew it. God knew it, and I didn't want to admit it. The worst part is, I allowed it to happen, and I had no one to blame but me.

After God revealed this to me the following week, I started to closely evaluate how overwhelmed by technology I really was. I quickly came to the realization that it was a lot worse than I originally thought. Denial. And I am not talking about the river in Egypt. I was spending all my waking hours—112 hours a week between my work and personal life—continuously exposing myself to various forms of technology. I was getting little to no downtime, I was only getting four to six hours of sleep a night, and, as if that weren't enough abuse, I was fueling my body with a constant intake of caffeine and fast food. Some form of technology was constantly stimulating me, occupying my time, and stealing my attention. I was tired. No tech-free elements existed in my life, and I badly needed a break from technology. Constantly feeling a sense of emptiness, stress, isolation, and a relational disconnect from my family and friends, it was time for me to take action. No longer could I deny it, ignore it, or avoid it. It was time to unplug my mind, restore my spirit, and transform my technology lifestyle, and so began my journey of creating a tech Sabbath habit.

Living Life in a Technology- Driven, Constantly Connected World

GLASBERGEN

"I just want a few minutes of peace and quiet — LEAVE ME ALONE!!!!!!!!"

"Technology now permeates American households and has become a central feature of families' day-to-day lives" so much so that we are no longer a society that just uses technology—we live it.[10] People of all ages continue to live their lives according to the rhythm and pace of the type of technology that is embedded in their lives. For example, if you own a smart phone or laptop, it is more likely than not that it is the center hub of your life's activities. It drives everything you do or don't do. You spend time with it when you are working or when you have free time and are relaxing or taking a break. It is the lifeline you rely on, and without it, you're pretty much lost. Or it may be social networking tools that drives your activities on any given day, who you hang out with, how you communicate with others, or what information you share. Whatever the technology is that is a part of your life, allowing it to enter your life without any boundaries puts you in a vulnerable position where you constantly find yourself worshiping at the feet of the god of technology.

As technology continues to become a larger part of our everyday lives, the risk of becoming overwhelmed by it increases, particularly for the younger generations (millennials, generation Y and generation X) who have no concept what life is like without it. Just over a decade and a half ago, much of the technology we have today was either in its early stages or did not exist at all. Life with technology was different. Mobile phones were the size of small bricks. Laptops were unheard of, for the most part, and social networking sites, texting, instant messaging, blogging, and Really Simple Syndication (RSS) feeds were not part of the social landscape.

Technology is in use everywhere and deeply engrained into most of our lives in one way or another. You can't get away from it. Everything from having the ability to carry the Internet in our pockets to HDTVs, microwaves that talk to us, refrigerators with TVs, programmable coffee makers, and electronic books that can be purchased and read online or downloaded to portable wireless devices. It follows us to school, to work, is with us in our cars and even when we go on vacation.

This technology-driven, constantly connected life where people are "always on" without any type of break from it—be it through their mobile phones, social networking sites, or smart phones—is really a dangerous place to live, and if not changed, the technology will slowly take over your life. Seeing the affects in my own life, including my kids and the people I meet everyday, the more technology that is consumed and embedded into our daily lives and routines without allowing ourselves to take a break from it, the more we are likely to sacrifice the things that matter the most to us—like our relationship with God, intimacy of face-to-face conversation, and the integrity of our relationships—for the things that matter the least, like the latest and greatest technology devices.

Ask yourself this question: As a result of the technology in my life, what more important things am I sacrificing by using it? My guess is that in at least one area, if not more, you are making sacrifices for things you shouldn't be as a result of your technology use. This whole concept of accepting technology unquestioningly into our lives and allowing it to rule us, rather than us rule it, has got to change. We cannot allow ourselves to be fooled into thinking we can't live life without it. The sad truth is that more often than not, we get so heads-down in technology that we forget what it is like to unplug and take a break, and then we end up losing perspective and focus. Our priorities get way out of order, and then we wonder why we have marriage problems, health problems, excessive stress, relationship issues, and experience varying degrees of isolation. For many years, constantly interacting with any kind of technology was my quiet coping device. It removed me from the world's problems. It gave me a sense of self-worth and self-confidence, and it ultimately became my place of rest. Now looking back during those times, to openly and willingly accept a technology lifestyle that drove me down a road of burnout, illness and fatigue, isolation, stress, strained relationships, and an absence of rest and relaxation, sometimes I wonder how I survived. Thinking back to a time where there wasn't as much technology, it is interesting to see how we managed our lives without it or used little of it and functioned just fine and were maybe less stressed. Nowadays, life seems to fly by at light-speed, and for some odd reason, we can't seem to live life without technology, and to even consider the concept of doing nothing is simply a waste of time. Even right now, you got distracted and probably feel that reading this book is wasting your time, and so you are thinking of setting it down so you can respond to a couple of text messages and check your e-mail. But resist the urge. It's okay. Learning to take back your life from worshiping at the feet of the god of technology is not easy, but the more we learn how to unplug and enjoy God's gift of rest, restoration, and rejuvenation, the more we can learn to transform our technology lifestyle to more of an abundant life we will be able to live and enjoy—the life that was promised to us by Jesus.

In John 10:10 (esv), Jesus says, "I came that they may have life and have it abundantly." What do you think Jesus meant when he said that? I am pretty sure we would agree that he does not mean for us to live a life overwhelmed by technology, filled with stress, frustration, isolation, burnout, fatigue, and health issues, right? In short, He promises us a life far better than we could ever envision. I find it interesting how we all get this false impression that we are living an abundant life by having all the luxuries of technology in our home, at work, and in school, but yet few of us are really living it. Why is that? Well, many of us allow technology and its luxuries to invade our minds, and we embed its portability and convenience as part of our normal everyday routines because we believe that life will be easier, better, more efficient, more productive. Realistically, the more technology we introduce into our lives without establishing clear and concise boundaries for its use, the more chance there is of it overwhelming our lives.

Sixty-three percent of parents who use text messaging believe that it improves their communication with their children[11], yet the number of minutes per week parents spend in meaningful conversation with their kids is three and a half minutes.[12] Did you know that the average person spends thirty and a half hours per month on their home computer?[13] That calculates out to be approximately 15 percent of our waking hours in a year are being spent in front of a computer screen. Seventy-two percent of Americans say they get excited or feel comfortable when they first use a new tech gadget. Five percent feel panic when faced with a new tech device, while 41 percent admit to feeling frustrated by their computers. In that same poll, the tech item that 54 percent of Americans consider a necessity is the mobile phone, followed by PCs (47 percent).[14] The Digital Video Recorder (DVR) was considered the third most essential item that people cannot live without. In the same survey, people indicated that DVR owners with partners say that having a DVR makes for a happier home life.[15]

When I read through these statistics and many others, God really helped paint the picture for me of how much technology is ruling our lives, and a lot of us don't even realize it or won't admit that it's true. The truth is that in order to live life in a technology-driven, constantly connected world, you must understand how to step back from it from time to time, take a rest from it, properly balance it, and control the use of it in your life. Then it will enhance life instead of overwhelming and ruling it. If not, the consequences can be severe and lead you down a path of emptiness, stress, isolation, and a relational disconnect from your family and friends.

When Does Technology Become Too Much?

DEAR, I THINK YOU'RE SPENDING WAAAAAY TOO MUCH TIME ON THE INTERNET.

I.COM
AM.COM
NOT.COM

© 2001 Randy Glasbergen. www.glasbergen.com

GLASBERGEN

In the early nineties, I remember my grandma and I talked about how much technology had advanced and changed since her time. She told me about how technology had made life far too easy for us, and as a result, people continued to overindulge themselves with it. She then made a profound statement that I will never forget: "People are over-indulging themselves in technology to the degree that they are losing touch with reality, and the basic skills of life are being lost due to this new technology-filled life." She further said that people didn't have to remember things anymore, everything was a convenience, people's manners had gone away, relationships and friendships were not being invested in, and it just wasn't healthy. Now keep in mind this was in the early nineties—a time when the technology advancements just really started to take off. She also mentioned that all this technology had encouraged and enhanced the laziness factor when it came to developing a good, strong work ethic. When I think about it now, I realize how true and right on target my grandma was. A lot of what she said has played out in my own life of which I am dearly grateful for. I have never forgotten this conversation, and I think back on it regularly and wonder, how much easier? How much more convenient? How much faster of a life do we need? How much more overindulging is it going to take before we get to the point where we say, "Okay, enough is enough"?

Today, eight- to eighteen-year-olds devote an average of eight hours to using entertainment media across a typical day (more than fifty-three hours a week). And because they spend so much of that time media-multitasking (using more than one medium at a time), they actually manage to pack a total of ten hours and forty-five minutes worth of media content into those seven and a half hours.[16]

The more technology we implement in our lives, the more dependent we will become on it. Is this a good thing? It definitely can be, only if the technology has a clear purpose in our lives, there are boundaries around its use, it does not steal our time, and it becomes a tool that enhances life rather than a leash that overwhelms it. When do you think technology becomes too much? How much of it do you need in your life before you draw the line in the sand and say enough is enough? Does it become

Bryan Brooks

too much when you choose to spend more time with your smart phone than you do your spouse? When things aren't going so well at home, do you turn to technology during those times? What about those times when you know you should be spending time with your kids, but instead you neglect them to spend time playing with the new technology gadget or gizmo you just purchased? How about those times when you waste time on the Internet serving your personal desires at work instead of actually working? Technology is too much when you allow it to consume your time and your thoughts and take over your life to the degree that, on a continual basis, you choose to sacrifice spending time and effort on the things of life that matter most for the things in life that matter the least.

Answer the following questions: Approximately how much time do you spend with technology of any kind on any given day? Approximately how much time do you spend nurturing and pouring into the lives of others or reading God's Word, exercising, volunteering, educating yourself, or pursuing a personal hobby? Figuring out your too-much threshold limit is critically important, because if you don't know where it is, you could end up in a detrimental position, jeopardizing important relationships, becoming socially isolated, or suffering health problems and other serious issues.

During my unplugging journey, I would go to great lengths to keep myself engaged with technologies of any kind. Until God revealed it to me in August 2008, I didn't have a clue that I even had a too-much threshold. My biggest indicator was that I was continually sacrificing things that shouldn't be sacrificed, such as spending time with God, my wife, my kids, and my personal friendships. My priorities were out of alignment. I didn't put God first. I would allow technology to interrupt our family meetings and dinner time. I would constantly reach for my laptop so I could see what was happening on various social networking websites instead of spending time praying over my wife for the things she needed prayer for or tending to her needs, nurturing, and valuing what God blessed me with. I would research unnec-essary new tech stuff on the Web, silently seeking out my next new tech toy purchase instead of spending quality time with my kids. I would consistently break promises and make excuses for why I couldn't participate in close relatives' events so I could play with my new tech toy. The list goes on. The good news is that the more you learn to recognize the signs, the more you will be able to prevent potentially disastrous situations from happening.

Bryan Brooks

Twenty-One Ways to Know If You Need a Break from Technology

"Our computer is practically like part of the family.
Maybe that's why it's so hard to get along with!"

With the plethora of technology to engage and overindulge in today, many people from different generations continue to experience the not-so-pretty side effects of technology, and the results are evident. Take a look around at the people you interact with on a daily basis. Look at how they use their technology and the impact it has on them. You will notice that they are addicted to their technology and, in most cases, they are completely oblivious to it. It's the intense screen-staring, mind-numbing, paralyzing state—you've seen it or lived it. But why do you think that is? It comes down to a couple of things. First, we all are in love with our technology. It fascinates and intrigues us. It is convenient, its cool, it gives us something to do when there is nothing to do, so much so that we treat it like a close pet. We feed it by updating it and storing information in it, we spend a lot of quality time with it, travel with it, and show it off like it is our prized possession. Once it becomes part of our life, we simply can't see life without it. Secondly, in most cases, there is lack of self-control, so it becomes a leash instead of a tool, and eventually it becomes the new idol, the new god, wreaking havoc on many important aspects of our lives.

When it is used as a tool that enhances our life, however, we are God-focused, have self-control over it, and know how it is implemented into our daily routine and life. Whether you have a little technology in your life or a lot, at some point, we all reach that moment in our lives when we just know that we need a break from it. Sometimes all that is required is a short coffee break for fifteen minutes or so and we feel great; other times a weekend getaway or sometimes a full-week vacation on a remote peaceful island is required.

In any case, regularly and consistently taking breaks from technology is important because your body needs it, and so does your mind. They both need restorative time. The less time you allow for this restorative process, the more of a dangerous situation you will find yourself in. I would never allow that break. I would exhibit clear signs and symptoms that I knew were not good, but yet I continued the behavior. I was stuck in a cycle of constantly and consistently overindulging and engaging myself and, at the end of the day, had no desire to change it.

In order to know when you need a break, though, you have to recognize the signs. In most cases, you won't recognize the signs, so you have to be willing to listen to the people in your life, family, and friends when they tell you that you are exhibiting these signs. They are a pretty accurate gauge and know when things are getting out of control. Then once you are made aware of the signs, it is your responsibility to do something about it. Take action and redirect your path.

Every one of us experiences different signs and symptoms. For example, I know I need a break from technology because I have a hard time focusing, I start to lose my patience, and I get easily frustrated and begin to feel overwhelmed quickly. I also notice that I have a hard time stepping away and will work hard to fulfill obligations, not because my heart is into it, but just because. Break time for me is stepping entirely away from the technology, listening to worship music, resting, or spending time with my family or with God. That is what I enjoy the most and gives me the most peace.

There are many different signs that can easily be detected when technology is starting to or has taken control of your life, which, in turn, indicates that you need a break from it. To begin with, we need to ask God to reveal those signs for us so that we can make the required adjustments to avoid the potential damaging effects on our lives. Secondly, we should listen to our family, friends, and those who care and love us the most. They have more insight and perspective than you realize. I can't tell you how many times my wife, kids, and friends made me aware of my technology issues and I just blatantly ignored them. Lastly, you need to take action once you are made aware of the issues. I just didn't care enough to change things until I starting suffering serious consequences. I don't recommend this approach. The list below identifies the most common ways to know if you might need a break from technology.

1. Predicting time is a problem for you. You consistently lose track of time when using your technology. For example, intending to spend an hour and, looking up, you discover it has been four or five hours.

2. Technology becomes your place of enjoyment. It becomes your place of rest and brings you a sense of excitement or happiness while using it.

3. You regularly lie and come up with excuses. You lie to your employer, family, and friends about your inappropriate and improper technology activities (e.g., online gaming, pornography). Even after experiencing consequences resulting from your inappropriate technology use, you continue your behavior.

4. You withdraw from real life. Hobbies, family get-togethers, hanging out with friends, as well as other social interactions and gatherings no longer become interesting to you.

5. You exhibit health-related issues more frequently than you expect. Things like carpal tunnel syndrome, eyestrain, weight gain, and backaches start to become the new normal.

6. You constantly get distracted and can't seem to focus on any one thing. You have difficulty having a face-to-face conversation with someone without some sort of technology creating an interruption that you feel is necessary to attend to.

7. Face-to-face communication and the personal one-on-one interaction is not attractive to you. You would much rather hide behind your technology by using text messages, e-mail, and voice mail when communicating.

8. You frequently miss or are late to important meetings, dates, and appointments. You allow the technology to disrupt your priorities.

9. You can't manage to leave home without it. You have your own technology bag where you bring several different devices and chargers when you go on vacation.

10. You can't seem to truly relax and wind yourself down. Some sort of technology ringer, reminder, or notification is constantly grabbing your attention (e.g., mobile phone call, voice mail message, text message, or e-mail).

11. Your family or friends ask you to stop, but you just can't seem to. You become irritated when others make you aware of your excessive use of technology, but you continue to ignore them and not recognize that they are trying to help you.

12. Technology becomes the priority over spending time with family or friends or other favorite hobbies/activities. You consistently miss out on important life moments and events. You pay more attention to your technology than what's happening in real life.

13. You spend more time with plastic and metal than with anything else. Nurturing, pouring into, and fostering actual relationships do not interest you.

14. Lack of sleep, resulting in grumpy, tired, and temperamental mood swings. If you're missing out on sufficient sleep—most likely seven to eight hours a night—you're probably irritable, dealing with mind fog, and have difficulty managing daily tasks.

15. You develop an alone feeling, although you communicate with people all day long.

16. You constantly talk about online or virtual friends whom you have never met nor intend to meet, but somehow your relationship with them is better than with your own friends and family members.

17. Technology becomes your coping device. It removes you from the world's problems. It gives you a sense of self-worth and self-confidence, and it ultimately becomes your place of rest and comfort.

18. You feel the need to check your mobile devices frequently during dinner times, family time, date nights, with your spouse, or playing games with your kids.

19. You get up in the middle of the night to check your mobile device if it goes off.

20. You go without eating on a consistent basis for several hours without thinking about it.

21. Your leisure time becomes a blurry, short-lived period in between work and personal time rather than a peaceful and restorative activity.

Bryan Brooks

The Keys: Three Things That Make Creating a Tech Sabbath Habit Effective

Unplug, restore, and transform—the perfect blend of simplicity to living a well-balanced technology lifestyle.

Whether you are already living a technology-enhancing life or in desperate need of learning how to live one, I encourage you to read on. This book is all about life-altering changes—not minor changes that go away after a few weeks, but changes that stick with you year after year. What you are about to discover in the sections that follow are the keys that make creating a tech Sabbath habit lifestyle so effective. All of these keys combined make up the lifestyle transformation that you are about to venture into. None of these keys are complicated and are profound life-changing tools.

Each key serves a different purpose. The first key focuses on severing the connection of technology inundating your mind. It breaks the constantly connected cycle by providing you with different techniques that will help you control what feeds your mind. Romans 12:2 (NLT) says, "Don't copy the behavior and customs of this world, but let God transform you into a new person by renewing your mind." In order to have a renewed mind, we must unplug our minds regularly and frequently and feed it things that renew and transform it. The second key is all about two words: *spiritual transfiguration.* Transfiguration, as defined by the dictionary, is a complete change of form or appearance into a more beautiful spiritual state. Psalm 46:10 (NIV) says, "Be still and know that I am God." In order to properly restore our spirit, we need to set down the technology, the busyness of life, and be still, learning how to quiet ourselves down and respect God's command of rest. We get that by spending Sabbath time with God and restoring, rejuvenating, and refocusing ourselves to our Creator. The third and final key focuses on overhauling your current technology lifestyle by teaching you new ways to set boundaries and help you better learn some etiquette when using your technology around others.

Key One
Unplug: Unplugging Your Mind

> When you unplug your mind, you develop a different attitude toward life; you can think more clearly, and you will instantly start to develop a more peaceful and serene spirit.

The sky's the limit when it comes to the overwhelming amount of technology that our minds get flooded with on any given day

Bryan Brooks

or week. Isn't it funny how sometimes we just feel that we are not doing enough unless every waking moment our minds are being filled with an activity? For many years, I always felt like, because of the technology in my life, if I was not multitasking, I was being irresponsible, and so I convinced and forced myself to multitask, even when I knew I shouldn't be.

How refreshed and rejuvenated do you feel after spending hours sitting in front of your computer, watching TV, surfing the Internet, listening to a talk radio show, or vegging out in front of a video game? My guess is that you're not refreshed and rejuvenated but probably more drained than you were before you started that activity. This is just one of many side effects that you will experience as a result of not unplugging your mind from technology. I experienced many of those days prior to and during the writing of this book and throughout my unplugging journey, and I can attest to the fact that now is the time to understand the importance of unplugging our minds from technology. The moment is here, and we need to take advantage of it and change our habits and lifestyle now.

What would happen if you were completely unplugged for one whole day? How would you feel? That means no technology of any kind. You're probably thinking, *Why on earth would I want to do that? That's dumb.* No, it's not really. In fact, there are many known side effects that can occur as a result of being exposed to prolonged periods of multitasking and technology stimulation. Never in history has the human brain been asked to track so many data points, and as an attempt to do more than what is possible, the brain paradoxically reduces its ability to think clearly.[17] Whether we are working or playing, we are tethered to our technology most—if not all—of the day. On the road, we listen to music or talk on our cell phones. At home, we have televisions, computers, video game consoles, Internet, etc. You need to spend time completely unplugging your mind from technology on a consistent and frequent basis. Unplugging your mind is important because it breaks the constant connection of information, disconnects you from your technology, and gives your mind a chance to restore, renew, and rejuvenate itself.

I remember many times in life when things would just get absolutely crazy and my grandma would say, "You need to disconnect yourself and get a change of pace." How true that is. What she was trying to get across to me was that I needed to break the cycle by doing something else. Let me encourage you and tell you that you need a change of pace. Right now! Today! Sometimes that is all it takes. We need to do something entirely different with no particular purpose, freeing our minds from the technology overload and the daily grind and business that life brings upon us. Here are some simple techniques that you can and should use regularly: Set aside time each day to take a short rest whenever or wherever you can. When you are eating breakfast, lunch, or dinner, don't do anything else. Enjoy your food, stop the media/technology intake two hours before bedtime, meditate on God's Word, schedule ten minutes a day as a mini vacation. Listen to music, meditate, or take a walk. Your body often gives out when it is exhausted; your mind acts in much the same manner. Give it some downtime from the daily commotion you encounter.

The Mind-Renewing Process

When you renew your mind, you renew your life.

The Bible recognizes that your mind is the gate through which you enter the world of positive behavioral change. Romans 12:2 (NLT) says, "Don't copy the behavior and customs of this world, but let God transform you into a new person by renewing your mind." You renew your life by renewing your mind. In order to have a renewed mind as scripture directs us to do, we must unplug our minds regularly and frequently from technology and feed it with things that help renew it. When you take time to renew your mind, it can result in a different attitude toward life;

you will be able to think more clearly, and you will instantly start to develop a more peaceful and serene spirit. The calmer and more serene you become, the better you will be able to handle the stresses of everyday life. Renewing your mind is important, and you should do it on a daily basis or as frequently as possible. There are many thought processes that control your mind. They have accumulated over many years, and in order to renew your mind and prevent your old thoughts from regaining entry, you must change your thought practices.

The Beauty of Living Unplugged Often

> The power is in the pause. Setting down the god of technology and living unplugged often brings back the beauty of life.

In the world we live in today, everything about our culture and the spirit of this age speaks against living an unplugged life. How long has it been since you took the time to just relax, take it easy, and unplug your mind from the busyness of life and the constant stimulation of technology for one whole day? If you think about this question for more than a few seconds, then it's not frequent enough. I know what you're thinking; *Bryan, there is just no way, with all that is going on in my life, that I can squeeze in any time to just unplug.* Believe me, there is a way. And even when there seems no way, there is still a way. Learning to be still is a hard enough thing to do by itself, but when we add the constant calling and distractions of technology, it seems like an impossible thing to do. In our culture, being truly still is almost unheard of and almost, at times, shameful. Culture continually shouts, "If you aren't doing something, you are wasting your time!"

Take something as simple as going on vacation *to spend time with our family members or loved ones.* We pack our laptop, smart phone, iPod, and all of our accessories so we can be entertained and connected. We book an itinerary so full most people feel they need a vacation from their vacation. But the purpose of unplugging is to recharge and reflect on our lives to do a pulse check on how things are going and ensuring they are going in the right direction—God's direction.

Jesus assures us there is a way in Matthew 19:26 (NIV): "With man this is impossible, but with God all things are possible." One would think that living an unplugged life in somewhat of a frequent manner would be fairly easy to do, and maybe for some people it is. If you're like me, though, it's definitely not easy. When I was going through my unplugging journey, I can remember many times where it created major stress and anxiety on me. That's because for so many years, I was so addicted to technology that when I didn't have it, I had major withdrawals, and it affected my emotional state. I became irritated, oversensitive, easily frustrated, and did not want to do much of anything. But through all of those emotional bouts, God—through His grace, love, and mercy—pulled me out of the pit of my spiritual enemy by exposing the many benefits that living an unplugged life often brings. This included things that I had been missing out on, like the simplicity of laughter, giving my wife and kids a hug, weekly family meetings where we talked about things going on in our lives, discussing the highs and lows of our days at dinner time, and many other things. It has other benefits too, like bringing back the beauty of life itself; providing calmness; reducing stress; giving you time to think; raising your energy level; encouraging activity, like going for a bike ride, hike, walk, or run; and helping build up relationships, because it frees up time for you to connect with friends and loved ones through socializing and shared activities. It's wonderful; so let me encourage you that taking this journey will help you get to a place where unplugging often becomes an important part of your life.

Bryan Brooks

Key Two
Restore: Restoring Your Spirit

Getting spiritually restored and strengthened in
God are vital to your existence.

The second key to creating a tech Sabbath habit is to restore your
spirit. This key is absolutely vital to your existence. When I speak
of restoring your spirit, I am referring to completely changing
your spiritual life. Transfiguration, as defined by the dictionary,
means a complete change of form or appearance into a more
beautiful or spiritual state. That's what we want—to restore spiritual beauty and be strengthened in God. There are many ways
to accomplish this, but the first and most important way is to
spend time with God. For example, this could include things like
spending time in His Word at least fifteen minutes at the beginning and end of each day, getting some degree of silence and
solitude with Him (i.e., praying)—even if its just five minutes
during the day—asking God to fill you up with His love and life
throughout the day or listening to worship music that draws us
closer to Him. This is a continual process and not just a one-time
event. If we neglect to prioritize time with God, then we lose out
on the powerful opportunity that God has given us because the
real power is in the pause. Setting down the god of technology,
taking a break, and infusing our bodies, minds, and souls with
spiritual food is mandatory.

Psalm 46:10 (NIV) says, "Be still and know that I am God."
Did you catch the first two words at the beginning of that scripture? God says, "Be still." This concept is huge and so important in today's society, where a lot of us find ourselves constantly
multitasking and jumping from one thing to the next. Satan, our
spiritual enemy, loves to keep us busy and steal our time so that
we feel we have no time for God or anything else that would help

us restore our spirits. A few ideas to restore your spirit might include cutting out things that hyper-stimulate you or reflecting and taking in the beauty of nature (either outdoors or through art, photography) or reading the bible or faith-filled books.

Keeping God and His Priorities at the Forefront of Your Life

There is great glory, favor, and blessings that come when God and His priorities are at the forefront of our lives.

God is not just another priority. He is *the* priority—at the top of the list. Number one. Scripture makes this quite clear in Exodus 20:3 (NIV): "You shall have no other gods before Me" and in Mark 12:30 (NIV): "Love the Lord your God with all your heart and with all your soul and with all your mind and with all your strength." That is the first and greatest commandment. When you place something else above God, that is idolatry. Idolatry is when you have extreme admiration, love, or reverence for something other than God (i.e. technology) But it could be anything.

When you have God at the forefront of your life, it is much easier to put everything else in place, for He gives us everything we need, including the strength to fight the good fight of faith, the love and devotion we need for our families and relationships, and the abilities, gifts, and talents that we have. God and the things of God are to be your priorities. One of the many results of putting God first in your life is that He will ensure your other priorities fall into place in their proper order, in a positive and helpful way. Putting any other priority in first place will only bring frustration, disorder, and chaos to your life. Unfortunately for me, what became most important was technology, and that took top priority in my life for many years. I would make it a point to go to great lengths to engage and indulge myself with technology, doing things like going into the bathroom at a restaurant so I could check my text messages without my friends or family knowing or pretending to go to the bathroom in the middle of the night just so I could do a quick check on my e-mail. But it could be anything from a workaholic nature to many other things. In some cases, we even go as far as establishing our priorities based on what will benefit us at the moment. (e.g., our job, money, promotions, social status, certain friends or acquaintances).

Setting priorities helps us clearly define our life purpose. To prioritize means to set things in order of importance. If we struggle in the area of prioritizing, we become ineffective and unfocused. With the demands in my own life, I find myself in this constant battle to keep my priorities in order and that the reasons are valid. Finances, work, family, entertainment, technology, pleasure, education, and a host of other "need to get done" things can also ruin your priorities as well.

Colossians 3:5 (NIV) says, "Put to death, therefore, whatever belongs to your earthly nature…" Proverbs 4:23 (NLT) says, "Guard your heart above all else, for it determines the course of your life". Your list of priorities will reflect what is in your heart. Matthew 6:21 (NIV) says, "Where your treasure is, there you heart will be also."

So how do we figure out what things in life are truly important? How do we discern what things are trivial or nonessential? We turn to God's Word. We seek wisdom and understanding. We get spiritual counsel, and we allow God to speak to us and direct our path in our quiet time with Him. Psalm 37:23 (ESV) says, "The steps of a good man are directed and established by the Lord when He delights in his ways." The best way to figure this out is to find out what is important and pleasing to God to determine what it is that He attaches special significance to and align our priorities accordingly. When God's priorities become your priorities, you will put Him and His Word first in your life. It's not an option; it's a necessity.

Another aspect of putting God and His Word first is putting His will first. If we are going to follow God's priorities, we are going to have to put His desires and His will for our lives over our own. The choice to put God's will for our lives first is a decision that we will have to reaffirm throughout our lives. The decision to do the will of God takes continual dedication and consecration; it's not just something we say to the Lord one time and that's it. He created you for a special purpose. You can trust Him to cause that purpose to be fulfilled in your life, and it will be better than anything you could have planned on your own. When we do this, we align ourselves with God's will, and our life priorities become much clearer. I refer to this as God's Priority Model, and it involves aligning your priorities with God's four key priorities. Let's take a look at each one of these steps in a bit more detail, for there is great glory in God's priorities.

Priority One: God

The first priority is your spiritual life. Scripture commands us in Mark 12:30 (NIV) to "love the Lord your God with all your heart and with all your soul and with all your mind and with all your strength." When God is first priority, we honor Him by doing the following: starting and ending each day with personal Bible study, prayer, praise, and worship; consulting Him with every decision and praying throughout your day (1 Thessalonians 5:17); accepting and acting on His Word (Proverbs 30:5); seeking Him first when our emotions get the best of us (i.e., when we are troubled, angry, worried, or frustrated) (Matthew 6:31-34); and choosing His way at every opportunity rather than leaning on our own ways and our own understanding (Proverbs 3:6).

Priority Two: Spouse/Family

The second priority is your spouse and family. To align with this priority and honor our spouse, we do the following: A married man is to love his wife as Christ loved the Church (Ephesians 5:25). Wives are to submit to their husbands "as to the Lord" (Ephesians 5:22). Husband is the head of the wife as Christ is the head of the church, his body, of which he is the Savior (Ephesians 5:23). To align with this priority, we raise godly children (Proverbs 22:6; Ephesians 6:4). Train our children up in the ways of God (Proverbs 22:6). Discipline our children (Proverbs 29:15).

Priority Three: Professional/Work

The third priority is to our professional and work life. Earning a living to support your family is important to God. Make sure, though, that God, your spouse, and your children have been properly and fully attended to before you focus on work. To align with this priority and honor our professional/work life, we do the following: Work hard for God. As you are working for the Lord, not for men, you know that you will receive an inheritance from the Lord as a reward. It is the Lord Christ you are serving (Colossians 3:23-24). First Timothy 5:8 (NIV) says, "If anyone does not provide for his relatives, and especially for his immediate family, he has denied the faith and is worse than an unbeliever." Another thing we must do to align with this priority is to get a job. If a man will not work, he shall not eat (Thessalonians 3:10). Be thankful for your job and enjoy it, but don't place your trust or devotion in work (Proverbs 11:28, 15:16, Proverbs 30:8-9).

Priority Four: Ministry/Church

The fourth priority is your ministry and church life. Notice that ministry is toward the bottom of the priority list, but that doesn't make it any less important. As a matter of fact, it helps put things into perspective even more. It's okay to guard our time, and it's okay to say no. Whatever you do, don't use the position of this priority as an excuse to do nothing for God or His local church.

To align with this priority and honor our ministry/church life, we do the following: Remember that you are fellow citizens with God's people and members of God's household. The church is an important priority in God's will for your life for a couple of reasons. First, what you're doing in the church of Jesus Christ is of eternal significance (Ephesians 2:19). Jesus said that the investment of your time, your energy, your resources here are laying up treasures in heaven, in glory. That's a dramatically different result from other pursuits in this life. Second, we need one other as we go through this life. We need to be with other believers where we can encourage and be encouraged, where we can give and be given to, where we can love and be loved, where we can serve and be served. We know that God's plan for our lives includes an important part to play in the church because He's given each one of us spiritual gifts for use in His church.

Key Three
Transform: Transforming Your Technology Lifestyle

If you think that you don't have a problem with technology but you spend every day with some kind of technology, you have a problem.

—Danielle Brooks

The third and final key to creating a tech Sabbath habit is to take your old technology lifestyle habits and transform them into a new technology lifestyle. It will give you more freedom than you ever had, save you more time, establish boundaries, and provide many other life-altering benefits. This key is paramount and involves a real paradigm shift in the way you implement and use the technology in your life.

Too many times we go out, buy technology, make it part of our lives, and just cruise through life, overindulging ourselves without realizing the impact on our own lives or those around us. For me, this key was hands down the most challenging. My wife, Karyn, can attest to the fact that when it came to my using or abusing of technology around her and the kids, it was pretty much a free-for-all, meaning that there were few boundaries around it in my life. Below are a few personal examples of bad technology habits that I was able to overcome and change. Maybe you can relate.

1. I would allow my smart phone or mobile phone to interrupt family dinnertime by responding to e-mails, phone calls, and text messages.

2. I would waste ridiculous amounts of time on TV, the Internet, in front of my laptop, playing with new technology toys of any kind, and blatantly ignoring my family.

3. I became so intrigued with new technology toys that I would stay up until the early morning hours (1:00 a.m., 2:00 a.m.) playing with it, knowing I had to work the next day.

4. I would always take some type of technology with me wherever I went, even if I didn't use it. It's the whole just-in-case mindset. I never wanted to feel disconnected from it. I was addicted to it. I felt weird if I didn't have it with me.

5. Technology became my place of enjoyment and rest. When I was looking to wind myself down for the day, I would turn to it every single time, rather than just resting, spending time with my wife, playing with my kids, or looking for other tech-free things to do.

6. I would allow technology to be used in our bedroom and the kids' bedrooms. Anything from DVD players to stereos and TVs. This caused major distractions to our family.

7. Cool technology and I were best friends. I had to have any new cool gadget that came out on the market, regardless of whether I could afford it or not. I cannot begin to

tell you the money I spent on stuff and how much stuff I accumulated over the years. Getting this under control was a huge deal and in the end saved our family massive amounts of money.

8. I am the type of guy who does not like confrontation, so anytime I got into a confrontation with my wife or kids, the technology became my coping device.

Understanding the Importance of the Sabbath

GLASBERGEN

**"Of course I brought it with me —
I still have 250 unused minutes!"**

Let's start at the beginning. God, the Creator who made all things—including you and me—fully understood the mind of man and knew both men and women would crowd their weeks with their own self-indulging activities. So He created a day and set it apart as a rest day. He actually commanded that man take a break each week. After six days of creating a wonderful world for man to dwell in (as well as creating man himself), we find that God rested from all His work.

> Thus the heavens and the earth, and all the host of them, were finished. And on the seventh day God ended His work, which He had done, and He rested on the seventh day from all His work, which He had done. Then God blessed the seventh day and sanctified it, because in it He rested from all His work, which God had created and made.

> Genesis 2:1-3 (NKJV)

In today's fast-paced, high-tech-driven society, we've forgotten an essential and important truth, which Jesus spells out in Mark 2:27-28 when he says that the Sabbath was made for man—not man for the Sabbath. He says that the seventh day, also called the Sabbath, was made for man as a time to take a break from our everyday routine, as well as a time to worship God.

When God gave Moses the Ten Commandments, one of those commandments (commandment four) deals directly with the Sabbath: "Remember the Sabbath day, to keep it holy. Six days you shall labor and do all your work, but the seventh day is the Sabbath of the LORD your God. In it you shall do no work…" (Exodus 20:8-10, NKJV) The Sabbath has two purposes: the rest and remembrance of God. It is the refreshing of your soul (your soul is your mind, will, and emotion).

When is the Sabbath? The Bible doesn't actually say what day it is; it just commands us to observe the Sabbath—a day committed to rest and worship. Without being legalistic about it, though, God meant and commanded us to take a day of the week and do no work on it. The Sabbath is a benefit as much as it is a command. God knows what you need far better than you do. Be still and allow God to speak to you in your time of relaxation and rest. You'll not only have more physical energy, but your mind will be more alert and creative, and your walk with the Lord will be greater. I don't guarantee it—He does.

Our culture is about distraction, numbing oneself; there is no self-reflection, no sitting still. It's absolutely exhausting.[18] Whether you realize this or not, there are great blessings in learning to unplug, slow down, and take a break. It helps to fight stress and gives the body a chance to recuperate. It gives you an opportunity to sit back, relax, and even to have the chance to watch a beautiful sunset without feeling guilty. You need a break. You need time set aside to take a deep breath and just relax. How bad do you want a break? Are you willing to accept the time God made for you to have a break? Is it important to you? It should be. It is important to identify yourself with the Creator of the universe.

God starts off the fourth commandment with the word *remember*. This is because He knew it would be lost and forgotten. God asks that we keep the Sabbath set apart for holy purposes so we can draw nearer to Him. The fourth commandment to remember the Sabbath concludes the section of the Ten Commandments that specifically helps define a proper relationship with God—how we are to love, worship, and relate to Him. It explains why and when we need to take special time to draw closer to our Creator and is also a special sign between God and us forever—that it is He who sanctifies us and Him alone we belong to and worship. The Sabbath, the seventh day of the week, was set apart by God as a time of rest and spiritual rejuvenation. Isaiah 58:13-14 (NIV) says:

> If you keep your feet from breaking the Sabbath and from doing as you please on my holy day, if you call the Sabbath a delight and the Lord's holy day honorable, and if you honor it by not going your own way and not doing as you please or speaking idle words, then you will find your joy in the Lord.

Learning to Slow Down and Create Margin

Margin and slow down—the two key ingredients to living less of a life of doing and more of a life of being.

Amidst the hustle and bustle of today's world and the technology that drives our lives, it leaves a lot to be desired when it comes to privacy and finding a moment to yourself, if only for a brief respite. Our high-tech world not only saturates us with all of its advancing technologies, but it also keeps us on tight schedules and has us multitasking more than ever, jumping to alarms, bells, and reminder alerts.

Living a technology-driven life that has no boundaries is becoming the standard, and it has to stop. God continues show me how powerful Satan can be about keeping us so busy and technology such a high priority that we almost can't see life without it. Ephesians 5:15 (NIV) says, "Be very careful (or culture will drag you away) then how you live, not as unwise but as wise." Let's be wise and not conform to the norm, if you know what I mean.

Consider these not so encouraging statistics: People now sleep two and a half fewer hours each night than people did a hundred years ago. You're sleeping less than your grandparents did. The average workweek is longer now than it was in the 1960s. The average office worker has thirty-six hours of work piled up on his or her desk. It takes us three hours a week just to sort through it and find what we need. We spend eight months of our lives opening junk mail, two years of our lives playing phone tag with people who are busy or who are not answering the phone, and five years waiting for people who are trying to do too much and are late for meetings. [19] More often than not, we are sleep-deprived, depressed, overstressed, and way too connected. A margin-less life creates stress and chaos, and technology does not help our cause. It leaves you vulnerable.

Here are a few examples of what happens when we continually live a margin-less life. Stress will rapidly increase. Your relational intimacy decreases (God, friends, family). Being too busy becomes the standard, and you adapt to and accept that the way you are living is the right way. You can live margin-less and be fine, as long as everything goes according to plan. But when the unexpected occurs, which it will, you don't have any space in which to fall. You move from barely hanging on to freefalling.

So what is the solution? The solution is creating margin in your life. Margin is breathing room and a little reserve that you're not using up. Having margin makes life more joyful. We become less anxious, stressed, and depressed and more relaxed.

While we always have a choice in how we react to life's snafus, it's much easier to maintain a positive mindset when we're not living so close to the edge. Margin has been defined as the space between your load and your limit. We're a piled-on, stretched-to-the limit society, chronically rushed, late, and exhausted. Many of us feel like Job did when he said, "I have no peace, no quietness; I have no rest, but only turmoil" (Job 3:26, NIV). Can you relate with that verse? Not having any margin is the new way of our culture, and it seems to be becoming the norm.

Bryan Brooks

Having margin is counterculture, having some space in your life and schedule. I once heard someone say, "The best things in life are found in the margin of your life." I will never forget that. I make a point to add margin in my life. Because of it, I have noticed that I am a much happier, calmer, and less anxious and stressed person. Margin is how you show yourself kindness. It's accepting that you can't do or be everything to everyone all of the time.

How do you get more margin in your life? The best way that I know of is to slow down. When you learn to slow down and begin to get more margin in your life, you will start to experience these immediate benefits:

- You will have a peace of mind. When technology is not driving your every waking moment and you're not hurrying and worrying all the time, you have time to think and process things, relax, and enjoy life. Peace of mind is having mental calm, serenity.

- You will have better health. Unrelenting stress resulting from technology harms our bodies. We all know that, yet we let it continue day after day. Many times the only time we get margin in our lives is when some degree of tragedy strikes. It's the heart attack that almost happens or the blood pressure skyrockets. Why do we wait until our health starts deteriorating before we make this decision? Why not realize that we need to build some margin into our lives now? The truth is that your body needs downtime in order to heal. Even racecars make pit stops occasionally to get repaired. You can't fix anything going one hundred miles an hour, yet we try to be repaired while we're still racing through life. Margin builds in time for better health.

- You will have stronger relationships. Lack of margin is one big reason for the collapse of the American family today. When we don't make relationships a priority and make time for each other, our relationships suffer. Relationships take time, and margin provides the time to sit and talk, to listen and enjoy one another, and to provide the comfort we each need.

- You will have usefulness in ministry. When you're over-loaded by activity, you can only think of yourself. You're in survival mode, just trying to make it through another day. But being available to God for His use makes all the difference in this world. When you have no margin in your life, when God taps you on the shoulder and says, "Hey, I'd like you to do this for me," your first response isn't joy. Your first response is, "Oh, no! Another thing to do! Sorry, God, I'd like to do that, but I'm just too busy." We end up resenting the great opportunities God brings into our lives. But when you have margin, you're available for God to use. When you have margin, you have time to be still and know that God is God (Psalm 46:10).

Another important part to fostering margin is that we must be able to find places where we can go on a regular basis and with-draw from all the technology—places that offer us spiritual ref-uge, renewal, hope, and peace. These places allow us to seek out and find the divine Spirit of the Lord. Mark 6:30-32 (NIV) says:

> The apostles gathered around Jesus and reported to him all they had done and taught. Then, because so many people were coming and going that they did not even have a chance to eat, he said to them, "Come with me by yourselves to a quiet place and get some rest." So they went away by themselves in a boat to a solitary place.

It doesn't surprise me that when Jesus saw the weariness of his apostles, the Lord not only told them to go away to a quiet place, but he also called them to be with him.

Getting away isn't enough. Resting and being alone far away from the crowd wouldn't rekindle the holy fire they needed. No matter how restful the retreat from the maddening rush may seem at the time, getting away by itself will not restore what is spent. Only the presence of the Lord can renew and restore our spirits. Here are some simple ideas to help create more margin in your life:

1. Take time to prioritize your life according to God's priority model. Without knowing and following God's priorities, we find ourselves chasing after many useless things that have little to no value.

2. Stop unnecessary time-wasters. Time-wasters are anything that decreases your productivity and effectiveness. Usually time-wasters cause a shift in your attention away from your top priorities. Many time-wasters are a form of distraction and interruption. Examples are things like watching endless amounts of TV, surfing the Internet for multiple hours a day, procrastinating, constant fire-fighting, lack of organization, etc.

3. Learn how to say no. Taking on too much adds excessive pressure and prevents you from working at your best. That means everything takes longer and more time is stolen. If you can't say no, it means you don't value your time, and you are allowing others to choose how you should spend it.

4. Give yourself extra time. Factor in the extra time it takes to get out the door to get to work early or on time, to make an appointment, or to pick up your kids from school.

5. Leave some space between items on your calendar/schedule. Don't run nonstop from one thing to another without any downtime.

6. Eat dinner earlier to allow for a relaxed evening routine. Hang out with your family before dinner, play a game, or sit and talk with your spouse.

7. Get up earlier to allow for a more relaxed morning routine. Start your day gently, rather than rushing about.

Keeping the Tech in Check: Setting Boundaries

GLASBERGEN

"With wireless sleep technology, the people
in my dreams can send e-mail and faxes
to the people in your dreams!"

With technology becoming more affordable, commonplace, and seemingly indispensable, its addictive potential is hard to deny, especially when it comes to setting boundaries around its use. According to a study by Lifewire, which included nearly five thousand Americans, more than 63 percent of smart phone users take the device into the bathroom. And 37 percent of laptop owners "frequently" use their computers in the bedroom.[20]

Setting boundaries is an issue of coming to grips with how to properly and politely integrate technology into our lives. It may also be similar to the sort of mentality that drives workaholics to neglect their families and personal relationships with the excuse of work so that they don't have to address the uncomfortable emotional issues they've left unresolved.

When it comes to setting personal technology boundaries and keeping them, it is not an option. They are important and necessary because it draws the line in the sand; it clarifies what we will accept and what we will not accept. It is the difference between what stays and what goes. It is focusing on the things that are important to us and setting aside the extraneous stuff. Boundaries are the dividing lines between what is good, safe, and acceptable and what is harmful and destructive. Boundaries that I find important to establish are date nights with my wife and kids, keeping my spiritual life in order through accountability partners, investing in important friendships, taking care of my health, and exploring new hobbies.

It's not new news that technology continues to invade our personal havens and negatively affects our sleeping patterns. This is primarily because a lot of technology ends up in places that it shouldn't, like in our bedrooms. For many years, there was a television in our bedroom, my smart phone was next to me on my nightstand, my stereo was on the dresser, and, periodically, I would bring my laptop into our bedroom to finish work-related stuff. Not good. This ultimately led to not only causing me to stay up later every night than I should have, but it also kept my wife awake as well, which shortened her night of rest.

It comes down to making healthy choices. You have to make the decision to keep technology out of your sanctuary, your haven. If you can't seem to achieve getting out of your bedroom, then turn the technology and lights off when it is time to go to sleep so your body and mind can get a well-rested night of sleep. By doing this, you might be surprised at just how great you feel, how much more energy you have, and how happy you will be after getting enough sleep on a regular basis.

Twenty-eight percent of Americans get eight hours of sleep on a regular basis, which is down from 38 percent in 2001. And two out of every ten Americans sleep less than six hours a night.[21] The risk of a fatal heart attack increases 45 percent in those who chronically sleep five hours per night or less. Sleep is a key ingredient to a healthy lifestyle; it affects your energy levels, your weight, your attitude, your mental functions, and even how your body functions. When you get enough consistent sleep, you are a healthier and happier person. The average adult needs a minimum of seven to eight hours of sleep each night to restore their body with the energy it needs to handle all of the demands of living each day.

Not getting enough sleep is more serious than you might think. Sleep-deprived people tend to develop more health problems, such as diabetes, obesity, and major illnesses, including cancer and heart disease. In fact, getting enough rest is imperative to living a healthy lifestyle, and when you do not properly relax and get enough rest, you are putting yourself at risk for illness, as well as other side effects. The amount of rest each individual needs differs. Also, when you don't get enough rest, you have difficult concentrating, thinking clearly, and even remembering things. You might not notice this at first or blame it on your busy schedule, but the more rest you miss out on, the more pronounced these symptoms become.

For a lot of us, life gets busier each year. Work, family, school, and other commitments eat the day away and leave you with little to no time to sit back and get some good old rest and relaxation. As you learn to consent to making rest a priority, a wonderful thing will begin to happen: You will find rest. True rest. Jesus said you would. In Mathew 11:29 (MSG), Jesus says:

> Get away with me and you'll recover your life. I'll show you how to take a real rest. Walk with me

and work with me—watch how I do it. Learn the unforced rhythms of grace. I won't lay anything heavy or ill fitting on you. Keep company with me and you'll learn to live freely and lightly.

Rest, with all it implies in terms of its fruitfulness, is worthwhile and satisfying in life. That is the secret of life. This is why Jesus says, "If any man will save his life, he shall lose it. But if he shall lose his life for my sake, he shall find it" (Matthew 16:25, Mark 8:35, Luke 9:24, NIV). He will find rest; he will fulfill the Sabbath, for that is what the Sabbath is. It is God's divine provision for us. In the only judgment that is ever worthwhile—the judgment before the assembled hosts of heaven when every life is reviewed as to whether it was worth the living, whether it hit the target or not—the secret of a success that will merit the words of Jesus, "Well done, good and faithful servant," is to learn the rest of God. Anyone who learns that (and to the degree that you learn it) is keeping the Sabbath as God intended the Sabbath to be kept.

Changing the What-I-Want-Is-What-I-Need Mindset

"It's an internet-ready, tri-mode, LCD color, MP3 compatible, digital wireless communicator. We make them extra big so people will notice how cool you are."

Not sure how much of a revelation this is to you, but technology marketing is a big business. In 2007, a forecast was made that US online advertising spending will nearly double by the year 2012, from $19.9 billion in 2010 to $35.4 billion in 2012.[22] That means more money, creativity, and time is being poured into developing various marketing strategies, tactics, and techniques every day, targeting consumers all to communicate the message of "What you want is what you need." It also gives the false impression that you need to not only be on the cutting edge of technology but the bleeding edge.

Consumer technology sales hit a record $129 billion in 2007, up 6.5 percent from 2006.[23] Technology marketing falsely leads people to believe that what you want is what you need. Most of us fall into the marketing tactics and traps by getting influenced by the right product, service, or device, if it is presented to us in a way that pretends to make life better, helps us fill a void, or prevents and or solves one of life's problems. Whatever it is that ends up flipping the switch inside of us to turn that want into a need is what heads us down the path of lack of self-control, impulse buying, and ultimately integrating technology into our lives that we don't need.

I know this is a simple concept to understand, but let's take a quick look at a couple of dictionary definitions for *want* versus *need* so that we can better understand the differences.

> *Want*: have a desire to possess or do (something); wish for.

> *Need*: require (something) because it is essential or very important, a necessity.

Being able to decipher the differences between a want and a need is important because once you're emotionally attached to the technology, it becomes difficult to detach yourself, and you end up turning that want into a need.

Let me give you an example of how this played out in my life. In October 2001, I heard about the first Apple iPod device. It sounded interesting to me to see, but it was not a necessity by

Bryan Brooks

any stretch, and I did not desire to purchase one. So on this particular day, I was surfing the Web and came across the MacWorld keynote address where Steve Jobs, Apple CEO, pulled an iPod out of his pocket and said, "One thousand songs in your pocket." Okay. Wow. It seemed like the strings of heaven started to play in my head.

Because I had previously developed an interest in my mind to at least see what it was about and what its capabilities were, I then went through a mock workup of justifying to myself in my head why I needed this iPod. It played out somewhat like this: "Wow. One thousand songs in my pocket...this iPod could do so much for me. It would virtually eliminate the need for all my CDs and my CD player, and being that I am a music fan of all types, I could literally take my whole music collection with me wherever I go..." *Wait*! *Stop*! That's all great and fine, but I don't need one thousand songs in my pocket, I never have needed one thousand songs in my pocket, and I still don't. But I convinced myself that it was a need rather than just a want. Not only that, but my friends purchased one, and that confirmed the fact that it was the cool thing to do. This type of lack of self-control is referred to in the Bible as a fruit of the spirit issue. God talks about this in Galatians 5:22-23, and the play on your emotions is exactly how we, as consumers, fall for the trap every single time. It is called technology marketing, and it tells us that what we want is not just a want, but rather it is telling us that what we want is what we need, and we need it now.

Have you ever bought a new piece of technology one day only to discover that the next day or the following week after your purchase that a similar piece of technology or even the same one is half the price with more features? Why is it that the technology available today always seems to be better than yesterday's technology? And what is it in our decision-making process or emotions that make us feel like we now have a void that never existed before? It is called technology marketing, and boy does it work.

What I can tell you, though, is that we must not look to technology or anything else to fulfill our voids, but we must look to God to fill them. If we allow our desires to be fulfilled by anything else, we will be let down every single time. Matthew 22:37-38 (NIV) says, "You shall love the Lord your God with all your heart, with all your soul, and with all your mind. This is the first and greatest commandment." God is commanding us to love him with everything we are, including our desires. If we look to fulfill our desires in Him, the urge to fill that void inside of us with anything else becomes no longer desiring.

For many years, technology marketing was like a starving fish yearning to satisfy his appetite with the right bait. It was one of those areas in my life where I knew that if someone could convince me enough times through different strategies, tactics, and techniques that my want for a specific technology was actually a need, then I would fall into the trap of purchasing things I didn't need and end up integrating yet another piece of technology in my life to occupy my time, stealing time from the precious things in my life—God, my spouse, kids, and friends.

Technology marketing is not a game; it is a serious matter. Listed below are some personal tips that helped me change the what-you-want-is-what-you-need mindset throughout my unplugging journey, and I believe you would benefit from them as well.

1. You always pay a price for technology. Let me say that again to ensure that sinks way down into your spirit—you always pay a price for technology! Anybody who tells you otherwise is lying to you. Technology, for many years, has been marketed as "This will make your life easier, and you are going to have more time to do the things you enjoy," and "I can fulfill and solve every need." The problem comes when you believe that and cannot exercise self-control. For most of us, the self-control part

is the biggest challenge, especially when we have a void in our lives that we are looking to fill.

2. What you see is not always what you get. Consider all of the details, read the fine print, ask questions. Make sure you completely understand what you are getting and what you are not getting. Otherwise, you will regret making the purchase, and you may risk losing your money. Also, read reviews about the product(s) you are buying and talk to friends who have purchased the same product and see how they like it and what some of the pitfalls are. Get wise spiritual counsel for big purchases!

3. Wait a minimum of twenty-four to forty-eight hours prior to making any technology purchases. The majority of the time, we make decisions based on how emotionally connected we are to a particular technology device or service. By waiting, the euphoria of your emotions tends to drop off, and you become less excited about the purchase and are less likely to buy. Figure out how much available time you have in your weekly schedule to spend managing another piece of technology. If you discover that you have very little or no time to manage another technology product or service, then don't buy it. It will be a curse to you rather than a blessing. Listen to your spouse if you are married; they are usually a good voice of reason. If you happen to be single, bring someone with you who has your best interest at heart. Many times, I have ignored my wife's instinct or opinion and, pretty much every single time, regretted the purchase that was made. Also, never move forward without peace. If you get an uneasy feeling about the technology you are planning to purchase, do not move forward with buying it. In the end, you will get buyer's remorse and regret the purchase.

4. Seriously consider what role the technology will play in your life. For example, if you buy a smart phone and you plan to use it for work, then use it for work purposes, not personal purposes. It is when you use technology to serve multiple purposes that gets you in trouble. It creates unnecessary confusion, like the never-ending workday because it blurs the separation of your work and personal life activities.

5. Limit your media exposure. Mass media promotes a spendthrift mentality. The more media exposure you consume through TV, radio, internet, etc., the more it influences your spendthrift mentality, which, in turn, results in convincing you that the technologies you have are not good enough and you should continuously upgrade.

The LG Syndrome: Avoiding the Temptation

When the latest and greatest technology temptation knocks at your door, remember the impact on
your loved ones, your life, and your wallet.

Let's be honest with ourselves. Be it a status symbol, the cool
factor, all of our friends have it, or the promise and provision of
its ease of use, comfort, convenience, and efficiency, we all have a
love affair with our technology to some degree. I will be the first
to admit that my desire for new tech toys has not entirely gone
away. After God helped show me, though, how much of a desire
I had and I acknowledged to myself and my family that this
desire was one of my biggest shortcomings that led to technology overwhelming my life; telling myself no; denying my selfish
fleshly desires; and avoiding the temptation to obtain the latest
and greatest technologies, whatever it ended up being, was one of

the hardest things for me to conquer. But I have conquered this shortcoming with the help of my family.

See if you relate to any of these questions: Have you ever had a burning desire to buy something new, better than what you currently have? Do you feel the need to be on the cutting edge of technology at all times? Do you have an incessant need to always try to impress people with your cool tech toys? Whether you answered yes to any of those questions or you were thinking that this could possibly be true, you may be suffering from a debilitating condition I refer to as the LG (Latest and Greatest) syndrome. For many years, I suffered from this debilitating condition. When I encountered a problem, confrontation, or had a void in my life that I was looking to fill, the solution I would turn to every time was to look for and get new technology. It's simply not worth it. Don't do it. Avoid the temptation. I know that sounds like simple advice, but I am speaking from experience. Not only does it cost a ton of money because you are paying double, sometimes triple, the cost but almost all of that cutting-edge technology, within a few short years, was half the price and did nothing long term to make life easier or more convenient. It just consumed more of my time and made me more frustrated.

The Bible tells us that temptations will come, and we must be careful not to walk in their path. Psalm 1:1 (ESV) says, "Blessed is the man who walks not in the counsel of the wicked, nor stands in the way of sinners, nor sits in the seat of scoffers." When temptations arise, remember that God has promised a way of escape for those who faithfully serve and obey Him. Sometimes the escape or way out can be obvious, like in Matthew 4:1-11, when Jesus fought back by quoting scripture when the devil tempted Him. Learn scriptures that pertain to your weaknesses and memorize them. Quote them often to yourself.

Other times, it can be the Holy Spirit talking to us. The Holy Spirit is our helper. Have you ever heard that small, quiet voice in your head that prompts you and says, "Don't buy that," or perhaps it's the voice that says, "Yes, do that with all your heart," or, "See that? So and so needs it. Buy it for them." Sometimes that voice isn't rational or doesn't make sense, but it is important to listen to it. The voice is the Holy Spirit talking to you. God gave us the Holy Spirit to help and guide us. John 14:26 (NIV) says, "But the Counselor, the Holy Spirit, whom the Father will send in my name, will teach you all things and will remind you of everything I have said to you." I've learned to be more open to what the Holy Spirit suggests. Over the last year, I've come to trust that voice and listen to it. It has helped me avoid the LG temptation many times.

When in doubt, we can ask the Holy Spirit for help: "Holy Spirit, help me make this decision. Should I or shouldn't I?" It's wonderful that God gives us the Holy Spirit to help us in times of decision-making. Romans 8:26-27 (NIV) says:

> In the same way, the Spirit helps us in our weakness. We do not know what we ought to pray for, but the Spirit himself intercedes for us with groans that words cannot express. And he who searches our hearts knows the mind of the Spirit, because the Spirit intercedes for the saints in accordance with God's will.

Practical ways to avoid getting LG syndrome are be content and thankful with what you have, for many times we are just not satisfied with what God has provided us with. Don't run out and buy new technologies just because you can. So many times we get hooked buying new technologies as a result of a sign, e-mail, or advertisement that we read or we hear about an awesome deal through a personal friend or the media, and next thing we know, we are purchasing that great deal. I got news for you. Deals will come and go all the time. If there is one today, there will be five more tomorrow that are much better.

Use what you already have. If you find yourself getting tempted to purchase new technologies, take time to go through your existing technologies and use what you have for a few weeks to curb your temptation. You may just discover some new features you didn't know existed.

Recognize your tendencies. James 1:14 explains that we are tempted when we become enticed by our own natural desires. The first step toward avoiding temptation is recognizing our human tendency to be tempted by our own fleshly desires. Temptation is a given, so don't be surprised by it. Rather, expect to be tempted. Be prepared for it. Pray about the temptation. Most of us know that any temptation can be difficult to overcome. In your prayer time, ask God to help provide you with the strength to walk away when you are being tempted. Use your Bible for inspiration. The Bible is filled with advice and guidance, so why not use it? Scripture verses like 1 Corinthians 10:13 (NIV), "You are tempted in the same way that everyone else is tempted. But God can be trusted not to let you be tempted too much, and He will show you how to escape from your temptation," can help inspire you in moments of temptation.

Give yourself alternatives. First Corinthians 10:13 states that God can show you how to escape from your temptation. Allow yourself to see that escape. If you know that technology tempts you, know how you can overcome it. For instance, if you know you are always tempted to purchase new technologies the moment you walk by an electronics store that is next to a grocery store you frequently visit, consider going a different route or maybe even finding a new grocery store that is not next to an electronics store.

Alternatives aren't always easy, but they can be the path God creates for you to avoid and overcome the temptation. It's not the end of the world. While avoiding temptation altogether makes life a lot easier, it can be discouraging when we do give in to that sin. We all make mistakes. That is why God offers us forgiveness. While you should not sin knowing that you can be forgiven, you should know that God's grace is available. First John 1:8-9 (NIV) says, "If we say that we have not sinned, we are fooling ourselves, and the truth isn't in our hearts. But if we confess our sins to God, He can always be trusted to forgive us and take our sins away," so you know that God will always be there ready to catch you when you fall.

Refocus yourself with praise. Praising God takes focus off yourself and puts it on God. You may not be strong enough to resist temptation on your own, but as you focus on God, He will inhabit your praise. He will give you the strength to resist and walk away from the temptation.

Repent quickly when you fail. The Bible tells us the best way to resist temptation is to flee from it (1 Corinthians 6:18; 1 Corinthians 10:14; 1 Timothy 6:11; 2 Timothy 2:22), yet we all still fail from time to time. We fail to flee. Notice I didn't say, "Repent quickly *if* you fail." Having a more realistic view— knowing that at times you will fail—should help you to repent quickly when you do. It is not the end of the world when you fail, but it is dangerous to persist in your sin. James 1:15 (NIV) explains that sin, "when it is full-grown, gives birth to death."

The Never-Ending Tech-Driven Workday

"Remember, for the next 2 weeks, *you* are on vacation — *but your Blackberry isn't!*"

When you look at the advancement and transition of technology in the workplace over the last decade and a half, most—if not all—of it is geared toward increasing productivity and efficiency levels. This is not a bad thing unless you find yourself becoming leashed to it. New studies are starting to indicate that technology is making workers feel more stressed, miserable, and less productive, especially mobile technology devices that demand urgent attention daily, even outside of working hours. It bombards our workday and continues to blur the separation of when the workday begins and ends.

In 2008, technology distractions in the workplace cost the American economy more than $650 billion in lost productivity and taking up 28 percent of workers' time. Mobile devices (laptops, smart phones, etc.) are the primary culprits, combined with the insatiable need to address and respond to electronic tasks as a result of being constantly connected.[24]

In March 2005, I got hired on at a major pharmaceutical company. As part of the job requirements, I had to carry a couple of mobile technology devices: a smart phone and a laptop. No big deal, right? Well, it wasn't at first, but what I noticed over the next few years was that it badly blurred the natural boundary that separated my workday from my personal time. Because I allowed that separation to become blurred, it put me in a jeopardizing position with my family because I would arrive home after a long day's work, looking forward to spending time with my wife and kids or even just resting a bit before family dinner time, only to find that my workday was not over. There seemed to always be something that required my attention. It could be anything from an urgent e-mail that required a response to work that required completion that evening for a next day morning meeting that I found out about last minute. So, of course, I would always do what any good, honest, hardworking professional would do: make the sacrifice, set my personal life aside, and take care of my work obligations, no matter what it took.

Over the years, this got really out of hand. I would usually start working around seven o'clock at night and would stop working around midnight or one in the morning, sacrificing my sleep, health, and time with my family. At first, I only worked these late hours about once a week. Then it was two to three times a week, then on weekends. Next thing I knew, it became my routine, and I was working almost every evening for several hours. What I discovered was interesting. First, I instantly noticed that my productivity level was higher, and secondly, I was more efficient because there were fewer interruptions and things to distract me from my work. But I also realized that technology became my ally at night for working in a distraction-free environment, and when I would go to work during the daytime, it turned out to be my main enemy. This caused major problems not only at work when I went into the office, as I would receive an influx of incoming calls between my office and smart phones, but there was also a constant flurry of e-mail messages in my inbox on my laptop, and text messages were frequently being sent to my smart phone for a variety of reasons. All of this made it extremely difficult for me to concentrate on a task and complete it in an effective manner. What bothered me the most was that I was selling myself out at the expense of the technology at whatever the cost. I had allowed my work and personal boundaries to get so blurred that it affected my health, my free time, and my quality time with my family.

The discovery of working late hours and the flexibility of having mobile technology devices, like a laptop and smart phone, does allow major flexibility—the flexibility to stay in constant contact and work whenever or wherever you want. These advantages cause many work professionals to take more of their work home. In fact, I have talked to many people in the work environment who end up feeling guilty for having abandoned their work obligations and responsibilities during normal working hours due to constant interruptions and distractions by technology, and then they get home and attempt to compensate and recover the lost time tenfold.

The advantages may seem helpful, but the underlying long-term consequences and detrimental effects on our lives are serious. For this reason, it is necessary to establish distinct boundaries around the modern mobile technologies that govern our personal and work lives so that we don't get caught up in the never-ending workday. Listed below are some key signs to watch out for, indicating that you could be caught up in the never-ending tech-driven workday cycle:

1. You allow technology to drive your priorities to the degree that you work outside of office hours on a regular and consistent basis.

2. You cancel dates with loved ones because your technology is constantly demanding attention, and you feel obligated to keep doing more work.

3. You postpone outings until you deem that the work deadlines are over, you are beyond exhausted, or you literally have information overload.

4. Because of the convenience factor, you take your mobile technology with you on vacation, and, as a result, you end up spending more of your vacation time doing work when you should be relaxing and unwinding. Your work goes everywhere, even to dinner with you.

5. As a result of being constantly connected through your technology devices, you continually try to do multiple things at once to keep your productivity and efficiency levels up. You set out to do one job and start on three more at the same time. But at the end of the day, you get very little done.

6. Your technology keeps you so occupied that you allow yourself minimal free time between work projects.

7. You work in the evenings during family time.

8. You allow phone calls, e-mails, and text messages to interrupt and lengthen your workday.

If you find yourself getting caught up in the never-ending workday cycle trap, here are some simple but effective ways to defend yourself against it:

1. Establish commitments that force you to leave work at a certain hour, such as meeting a friend, a doctor or dentist appointment, or having to go pick up the kids at school.

2. Saying no acts as a repellant substance. As hard as it is sometimes, we just need to learn to say no. Having clear objectives in both your professional and personal life helps separate between the commitments we can accept and the ones to reject.

3. Learn to use the power-off button and turn off the technology. Sometimes we forget, but all technology devices come with an off button, and we've got to figure out where it is and use it once in a while.

4. Don't let working late hours become commonplace. Every now and again, you may have to work a few late hours for a short period of time to get a project finished, but it is not necessary to work late hours on a regular basis. During your free time after the workday has ended, some things you could do are: take time to play some games with your kids, take a stroll in the park or around your neighborhood, walk your dog, go see a favorite band you like in concert, take a bike ride, finish up a hobby project you started or start something new, read some books, take your spouse on a date to a nice restaurant, or just kick back and rest.

The Tech Sabbath Habit Journey

Creating a tech Sabbath habit in your life will help you discover something new in the pause—the things in life that truly matter.

I once heard a profound saying that I will never forget: "On the keyboard of life, always keep one finger on the escape key." It continually reminds me of times in my life when I had intentionally taken the time to get away and get some solitude, peace, and rest. I can't begin to tell you how many years, moments, and opportunities I had to do so but chose not to take advantage of them.

Take a moment and imagine this with me: A peaceful, restful, and relaxing getaway without technology of any kind. Just you and some close friends or your family enjoying lots of sunsets, days of breathing deeply, plenty of good food and drink, lots of laughter, and fun times. Sounds good, yeah? Well it is, and let me encourage you to make the time to do this regularly, wherever that may be, because if you never allow yourself to get away and take a break periodically—not just from technology but anything—you will live a frustrated, chaotic, and stress-filled life. You need an opportunity to just step away and take in the beauty of life—God's creation.

In order to create a tech Sabbath habit lifestyle, it takes consistent practice, patience, and persistence on your part, as with anything in life you take on. As you are going to experience by going through each week of the journey, life can be enjoyable when you are not letting it control your life. A lot of us don't allow ourselves to properly rest and relax, but when you're unplugged, you have no choice but to enjoy and savor each moment that life brings. Before going through the journey, I want to share a few tips with you that helped me remain successful and committed to it.

- Take action, no matter how you feel. A lot of times we allow our emotions and feelings to get in the way, especially when we get discouraged or fail at something. So try your best to take action! It will pay off!

- Choose to look at change with a new perspective so that any change becomes a good change. Dealing with any change always presents a challenge.

- Focus on the benefits! You will experience some degree of withdrawal pain at first, but it is important to focus on the benefits you are receiving as a result of the change and not the withdrawal pain. God is with you, so who can be against you?

- You are powerful, and you can change your life. The reality is that you can discover new ways to enjoy your newly transformed life.

- Be optimistic and keep a positive attitude! As you go through the journey, your attitude makes a world of difference. Stay positive. Try to hang around people who encourage you and want you to succeed.

- Protect your tech Sabbath habit day. Tell people about your day off and why it is important to you, celebrate what you do with your time off, ask others what they do with their days off, and, at all costs, avoid technology.

Before beginning, I assembled a quick overview of the tech Sabbath habit process steps. These steps will help you gain a better understanding of how to complete the weekly plans. The weekly plan format is intentionally simple and easy to follow. There are five basic steps that you will complete each week, they are:

- Step 1 – Kick off the week by selecting which day will be earmarked as your "tech-free" day by circling it in the plan. Keep in mind that it doesn't have to be a certain day of the week; it can fluctuate from week to week, however it fits into your schedule.

- Step 2 - Jump right into the first part of the plan by reading the encouraging thought of the week and then complete the technology challenge and "taking action" step for that week.

- Step 3 – As you progress throughout the week in your normal routine, just live your current technology lifestyle as you normally would. Be honest with yourself, and each day, for the hours you are awake, record the amount of time you spend with technology and without it on the time recording table.

- Step 4 – On "tech-free" day, start by first completing these three unplugging/restoring activities:

  a. Find a quiet place where there will be no interruptions or distractions, sit down, grab your Bible or devotional or read encouraging, inspiring, faith-filled books for fifteen minutes at the beginning of your day.

  b. Dedicate one hour to clear your mind by doing absolutely nothing but rest.

  c. Elevate your mood by going outside and taking a walk or just hang out in the beauty of nature—God's creation.

- Step 5 – On "tech-free" day, choose activity ideas listed under the "Transforming Activities" section of the plan and fill your day with as many of them as possible or feel free to make up your own, if you so desire. The goal is to avoid technology at all costs on this day.

Tech Sabbath Habit Plan: Week 1

This week, my tech-free day is (circle one):

Mon Tues Wed Thurs Fri Sat Sun

This week's encouraging thought: Never let the word *"impossible"* stop you from pursuing what your heart and spirit tell you to do. Impossible things come true every day.

This week's technology challenge: Gain control over the amount of software-related technology tools in your life. This would include things like too many e-mails, instant messages, social networking accounts, etc. If you are the type of person who has four instant messaging accounts, three social networking profiles, and five e-mail addresses (four of which you rarely use or not at all), that is too much. The more time you spend managing unnecessary software-related tools, the less time you have to spend on the things that really matter, like a hobby you have been wanting to pursue, personal goals you have been wanting to accomplish (e.g., going back to school, traveling the world), or investing in friendships, family relationships, and growing your relationship with God.

Taking action: This week, identify and list out the total number of e-mail accounts, instant messaging accounts, social networking and professional networking accounts, or other accounts you have accumulated. Once you have identified how many you have, carefully evaluate each one and determine its importance to your life. Eliminate ones that are truly not a necessity to have and are just time-wasters. A good indication for this is that if you don't log in to the account at least weekly, it is probably something that is really not necessary to have.

As you progress throughout the week, record the time you spent with technology and without it.

Bryan Brooks

Day	Date	Awake Time	Sleep Time	Technology Time		Tech-Free Time	
				Hours	Minutes	Hours	Minutes
		16 Hours	8 Hours				
		16 Hours	8 Hours				
		16 Hours	8 Hours				
		16 Hours	8 Hours				
		16 Hours	8 Hours				
		16 Hours	8 Hours				
		16 Hours	8 Hours				
Totals		112 Hours	56 Hours				

Transforming Activities

Activity ideas: Sit and take in a nice sunrise or sunset, go to a baseball game, go to the playground at a nearby park, spend time with friends. Invite someone new to lunch, welcome and get to know new-hires at your work. When a coworker needs to talk, meet him or her at lunch and listen with compassion. Say something nice to everyone you meet today, give the gift of your smile, volunteer at your local church or an agency that needs help.

Other activities:

_____

_____

Tech Sabbath Habit Plan: Week 2

This week, my tech-free day is (circle one):

Mon Tues Wed Thurs Fri Sat Sun

This week's encouraging thought: Change only occurs when the pain of not changing becomes too great.

This week's technology challenge: Pay attention to warning signs your body is alerting you to when using technology. Don't ignore them! Warning signs our bodies give us are accurate indicators that something is not right. It is important that we pay attention to them and take the appropriate action steps to avoid them from reoccurring—things like red, hurting, dry eyes; a splitting headache after staring at technology devices for four hours straight; lower back pain from sitting in an improper position when using our laptop; or excessive consumption of caffeinated drinks and/or eating vending machine snacks or fast food because of our busy tech-driven lifestyle.

Taking action: This week, pay attention to how you are feeling when using technology. Because technology can be so mind numbing and paralyzing, it's easy to ignore warning signs that our bodies are experiencing and keep on going. Pay attention and take charge! Change your eating habits. Don't eat fast food or snacks from vending machines, and avoid energy or heavily caffeinated drinks. Take short breaks where you get a chance to take a few deep breaths throughout the day, and maintain good seating posture if you do have to sit for long periods of time in front of technology devices. To avoid putting undue strain on your eyes, take frequent mini breaks where you can look away; don't constantly stare at your smart phone device, computer, or iPod screen.

As you progress throughout the week, record the time you spent with technology and without it.

Bryan Brooks

Day	Date	Awake Time	Sleep Time	Technology Time		Tech-Free Time	
				Hours	Minutes	Hours	Minutes
		16 Hours	8 Hours				
		16 Hours	8 Hours				
		16 Hours	8 Hours				
		16 Hours	8 Hours				
		16 Hours	8 Hours				
		16 Hours	8 Hours				
		16 Hours	8 Hours				
Totals		112 Hours	56 Hours				

Transforming Activities

Activity ideas: Love more, dream more, take dancing lessons with your spouse, and go see a theater play. Ride on a zip line, ride a camel or an elephant, become proficient at origami, go deep sea fishing, go to an underwater aquarium, watch a space shuttle launch. Have a barbecue with coworkers, tell your boss why you appreciate him or her, and remember others' birthdays and important events. Work in a concession stand to raise money for a good cause, volunteer to help with a local event in your area, volunteer to be a museum guide.

Other activities:

_____

_____

Tech Sabbath Habit Plan: Week 3

This week, my tech-free day is (circle one):

Mon Tues Wed Thurs Fri Sat Sun

This week's encouraging thought: Life transformation is rooted in mind transformation.

This week's technology challenge: Limit your television consumption and set rules around its use. One of the easiest ways to fall into the trap of watching too much TV is through lack of attention, our own loneliness, or using it as a babysitting tool or as a mechanism for rest and relaxation. In 2008, Americans watched 151 hours of television per month.[25] That means 30 percent of our time is being spent watching TV. Forty-nine percent of kids ages two to eighteen watch TV with no rules around its use.

Taking action: This week, limit your TV watching to only two hours a day. Set a timer to keep track for yourself and your family and stick to it.

As you progress throughout the week, record the time you spent with technology and without it.

Bryan Brooks

Day	Date	Awake Time	Sleep Time	Technology Time		Tech-Free Time	
				Hours	Minutes	Hours	Minutes
		16 Hours	8 Hours				
		16 Hours	8 Hours				
		16 Hours	8 Hours				
		16 Hours	8 Hours				
		16 Hours	8 Hours				
		16 Hours	8 Hours				
		16 Hours	8 Hours				
Totals		112 Hours	56 Hours				

Transforming Activities

Activity ideas: Visit the state or county fair, start a scrapbook and fill it with items found outdoors, have a campfire in your backyard, roast marshmallows. Tour a firehouse or police station, go bowling, refrain from negative talk, concentrate on the positive, show your appreciation to coworkers through words and notes. Mentor junior high or high school exchange students, read books to children in medical clinics or your local library, teach an adult to read, participate in coastal cleanup day.

Other activities:

_____

_____

Tech Sabbath Habit Plan: Week 4

This week, my tech-free day is (circle one):

Mon Tues Wed Thurs Fri Sat Sun

This week's encouraging thought: When the world says, "Give up," hope whispers, "Try it one more time."

This week's technology challenge: Learn to turn off your mobile technology devices prior to a meeting or engaging in conversation with others. Not vibrate or quiet mode—totally off. It shows respect and that you care. Not turning off your mobile technology devices is just downright rude, inconsiderate, and is distracting to others. Mobile technology devices and their convenient features continue to create the perception and expectation that we can be interrupted from anything at any time and be available at all times.

Taking action: This week, turn off your mobile technology devices prior to a meeting or engaging in a conversation. All mobile technology devices are designed with a power off button, so find out where it is on your device and use it once in a while. It will be refreshing. People will admire and respect you for it.

As you progress throughout the week, record the time you spent with technology and without it.

Bryan Brooks

Day	Date	Awake Time	Sleep Time	Technology Time		Tech-Free Time	
				Hours	Minutes	Hours	Minutes
		16 Hours	8 Hours				
		16 Hours	8 Hours				
		16 Hours	8 Hours				
		16 Hours	8 Hours				
		16 Hours	8 Hours				
		16 Hours	8 Hours				
		16 Hours	8 Hours				
Totals		112 Hours	56 Hours				

Transforming Activities

Activity ideas: Play Twister, jog at sunset, join a health club. Have a water balloon fight, play board games by a toasty fire, build a model car or airplane. Leave a treat on the desk of a coworker with whom you normally don't get along with; write, draw, make, or buy something encouraging for a colleague who is experiencing difficulties; offer to babysit a coworker's children for an evening. Get involved by leading a campaign to eliminate world famine, help terminally ill people by tending to their needs.

Other activities:

_____

_____

Tech Sabbath Habit Plan: Week 5

This week, my tech-free day is (circle one):

Mon Tues Wed Thurs Fri Sat Sun

This week's encouraging thought: Value even the smallest moments of inspiration.

This week's technology challenge: Don't waste time on the Internet. The Internet is the ultimate time-waster and can be a huge distraction. Social isolation continues to increase, and the Internet is a major contributor to this isolation. The fact is that the Internet is a great, powerful tool for many reasons (research, current news, etc.). But at the same time, there is a lot of unnecessary information that we end up filling our minds with. Wasting time on the Internet is a strong indication that you are bored and need something more productive to do.

Taking action: This week, stay off the Internet if you are bored and looking to just waste time. Have a clear purpose for using it if you don't just avoid it.

As you progress throughout the week, record the time you spent with technology and without it.

Bryan Brooks

Day	Date	Awake Time	Sleep Time	Technology Time		Tech-Free Time	
				Hours	Minutes	Hours	Minutes
		16 Hours	8 Hours				
		16 Hours	8 Hours				
		16 Hours	8 Hours				
		16 Hours	8 Hours				
		16 Hours	8 Hours				
		16 Hours	8 Hours				
		16 Hours	8 Hours				
Totals		112 Hours	56 Hours				

Transforming Activities

Activity ideas: Call your spouse just to say I love you or to tell him or her what you appreciate about them. Take up a hobby, such as playing an instrument or drawing. Be open to establishing friendships with coworkers you have never met before, take a class that is related to the work you do, go back to school. Take retreats, go on mission trips to other nations or countries, and minister to someone using your gifts. Read inspirational books, assist with craft preparations for child story time, or offer to volunteer at your local library.

Other activities:

_____

_____

Tech Sabbath Habit Plan: Week 6

This week, my tech-free day is (circle one):

Mon Tues Wed Thurs Fri Sat Sun

This week's encouraging thought: Know you were born an original to make a difference in the world.

This week's technology challenge: Don't allow and accept constant technology interruptions or disruptions. In our fast-paced, multitasking, super-busy lives we lead, the little bit of quality time we do get needs to be highly valued, nurtured, and cherished.

Taking action: This week, do not allow or accept technology interruptions during family time or quality time with your spouse, friends, or kids. The easiest way to not allow technology to interrupt or disrupt is to turn it off. If turning it off is not possible, then try silencing or muting it.

As you progress throughout the week, record the time you spent with technology and without it.

Day	Date	Awake Time	Sleep Time	Technology Time		Tech-Free Time	
				Hours	Minutes	Hours	Minutes
		16 Hours	8 Hours				
		16 Hours	8 Hours				
		16 Hours	8 Hours				
		16 Hours	8 Hours				
		16 Hours	8 Hours				
		16 Hours	8 Hours				
		16 Hours	8 Hours				
Totals		112 Hours	56 Hours				

Transforming Activities

Activity ideas: Go whitewater rafting, ride a horse on the beach, laugh out loud. Crank up some music, get a Tootsie Pop and see how many licks it takes to get to the center. Help those at work who have difficulties performing their work, bring treats to share with coworkers, give a compliment, help an overworked colleague with tasks. If you have swimming skills and experience, volunteer as a lifeguard at the community public pool; volunteer to be an after-school tutor; volunteer to help out seniors in your neighborhood with tasks that they are unable to perform.

Other activities:

_____

_____

Tech Sabbath Habit Plan: Week 7

This week, my tech-free day is (circle one):

Mon Tues Wed Thurs Fri Sat Sun

This week's encouraging thought: Why not learn to enjoy the little things? There are so many of them.

This week's technology challenge: Stop the technology activity two hours before you plan to go to bed. By doing this, your mind and body will settle down and unwind from the day. When we do not allow for this unwinding period, the outcomes can lead to things like the lack of the proper amount of sleep (minimally seven to eight hours), constant interruption of our sleep, undue emotional stress because of what our minds are filled with, late-night eating, etc.

Taking action: This week, stop the technology activity and interaction two hours before bedtime.

As you progress throughout the week, record the time you spent with technology and without it.

Bryan Brooks

Day	Date	Awake Time	Sleep Time	Technology Time		Tech-Free Time	
				Hours	Minutes	Hours	Minutes
		16 Hours	8 Hours				
		16 Hours	8 Hours				
		16 Hours	8 Hours				
		16 Hours	8 Hours				
		16 Hours	8 Hours				
		16 Hours	8 Hours				
		16 Hours	8 Hours				
Totals		112 Hours	56 Hours				

Transforming Activities

Activity ideas: Go camping, go for a hike in the woods, go fishing, go for a swim, have a carpet picnic, work on an arts and craft project. Offer to help out with the not-so-pleasant tasks at work, write a letter commending an employee who helped you and address it to his or her boss, teach one of your skills to another coworker, and learn a skill from him or her as well. Donate books; donate goodies for children to deliver to city service workers, volunteer at a health fair or as a camp counselor for a youth camp.

Other activities:

_____

_____

Tech Sabbath Habit Plan: Week 8

This week, my tech-free day is (circle one):

Mon Tues Wed Thurs Fri Sat Sun

This week's encouraging thought: You'll never change your life until you change your choices.

This week's technology challenge: Limit your time on social networking websites to one hour each day this week. There is a lot to love about social networking websites. They help to keep us in touch with friends and family because we can chat to each other in real time and share photos and videos all at the click of a mouse button. However, all social networking sites draw you in, and next thing you know, you are spending (wasting) more time there than you intended on spending. These sites can be entertaining, fun, and addicting; however, they are a huge draw on your free time.

Taking action: This week, set a time limit of no more than one hour each day on social networking websites. Set a timer and keep track. Ask a family member, your spouse, or a close friend to help you stay accountable.

As you progress throughout the week, record the time you spent with technology and without it.

Bryan Brooks

Day	Date	Awake Time	Sleep Time	Technology Time		Tech-Free Time	
				Hours	Minutes	Hours	Minutes
		16 Hours	8 Hours				
		16 Hours	8 Hours				
		16 Hours	8 Hours				
		16 Hours	8 Hours				
		16 Hours	8 Hours				
		16 Hours	8 Hours				
		16 Hours	8 Hours				
Totals		112 Hours	56 Hours				

Transforming Activities

Activity ideas: Go mountain biking or whitewater rafting, play cards, climb a tree, make a rope swing, jump on a trampoline. Leave a treat on the desk of a coworker with whom you normally don't get along; write, draw, make, or buy something encouraging for a colleague who is experiencing difficulties. Offer to babysit a coworker's children for an evening. Participate in a clothes trading program or event for the less fortunate. Help set up a bulletin board to help arrange carpools for people in your community. Offer your services to a ministry.

Other activities:

_____

_____

Tech Sabbath Habit Plan: Week 9

This week, my tech-free day is (circle one):

Mon Tues Wed Thurs Fri Sat Sun

This week's encouraging thought: A word of love can make a world of difference.

This week's technology challenge: Do not turn to technology when you get time to unwind and relax. Avoid using it as a relaxation mechanism. For a lot of us who use technology on a regular basis, whether for work or personal reasons, it is the thing we immediately turn to when we need a relaxing moment, and then it ends up that we can't seem to get any true relaxation without it. Instead, grab your favorite book, novel, or magazine; sit and rest; or spend time with your friends or family instead.

Taking action: This week, when you get the urge to relax, don't turn to technology—avoid it entirely. Find another outlet or source that does not involve or require it.

As you progress throughout the week, record the time you spent with technology and without it.

Bryan Brooks

Day	Date	Awake Time	Sleep Time	Technology Time		Tech-Free Time	
				Hours	Minutes	Hours	Minutes
		16 Hours	8 Hours				
		16 Hours	8 Hours				
		16 Hours	8 Hours				
		16 Hours	8 Hours				
		16 Hours	8 Hours				
		16 Hours	8 Hours				
		16 Hours	8 Hours				
Totals		112 Hours	56 Hours				

Transforming Activities

Activity ideas: Do some bird watching, visit a vineyard—some tours are free while others are affordable—visit a street fair. Rollerblade, take a ride on an electric scooter, visit the zoo. Bring in a treat to share with coworkers, give a compliment, and help an overworked colleague with some tasks. Discover your gifts, talents, and abilities and use them to serve others or the local church (i.e., be a small group leader, serve on a media team, become an altar worker, kids church)

Other activities:

_____

_____

Tech Sabbath Habit Plan: Week 10

This week, my tech-free day is (circle one):

Mon Tues Wed Thurs Fri Sat Sun

This week's encouraging thought: Eliminate everything unnecessary in your life in order to put first things first.

This week's technology challenge: Reduce your exposure to technology advertising. Technology advertising makes us believe that what we want is actually what we need, and, in turn, it makes us desire things more. Taking action: This week, do whatever it takes to reduce your exposure to different forms of technology advertising. Turn off the TV, ignore the ads in your favorite magazine, change the channel on your radio—do whatever is necessary to avoid it.

As you progress throughout the week, record the time you spent with technology and without it.

Bryan Brooks

Day	Date	Awake Time	Sleep Time	Technology Time		Tech-Free Time	
				Hours	Minutes	Hours	Minutes
		16 Hours	8 Hours				
		16 Hours	8 Hours				
		16 Hours	8 Hours				
		16 Hours	8 Hours				
		16 Hours	8 Hours				
		16 Hours	8 Hours				
		16 Hours	8 Hours				
Totals		112 Hours	56 Hours				

Transforming Activities

Activity ideas: Visit historic battlefields; take a day trip to Washington, DC, where most of the museums are free; teach yourself a new language using materials from the library. Visit a dairy farm; have a scavenger hunt. Place a flower on the desk of each of your coworkers; put an anonymous, supportive note on an employee's desk; contribute to a good news bulletin board. Volunteer to visit high school classes and talk about your work responsibilities.

Other activities:

_____

_____

Tech Sabbath Habit Plan: Week 11

This week, my tech-free day is (circle one):

Mon Tues Wed Thurs Fri Sat Sun

This week's encouraging thought: The dreams of your future have no room for the devastations of your past.

This week's technology challenge: Create clear boundaries between your work and personal mobile technology devices by removing e-mail, instant messaging, or social networking accounts that are not necessary to be on there. Allowing these things on your work mobile device blurs the separation between your personal and professional life which creates unnecessary confusion about when your professional workday ends and your personal life begins. Strive to create separation.

Taking action: This week, remove any personal e-mail, instant messaging, or social networking accounts from your work mobile device, and do the same for your personal mobile device—remove any work e-mail, instant messaging, or social networking accounts.

As you progress throughout the week, record the time you spent with technology and without it.

Day	Date	Awake Time	Sleep Time	Technology Time		Tech-Free Time	
				Hours	Minutes	Hours	Minutes
		16 Hours	8 Hours				
		16 Hours	8 Hours				
		16 Hours	8 Hours				
		16 Hours	8 Hours				
		16 Hours	8 Hours				
		16 Hours	8 Hours				
		16 Hours	8 Hours				
Totals		112 Hours	56 Hours				

Transforming Activities

Activity ideas: When your coworkers have a tight deadline to meet and it looks like they may not make it, ask them if you can help, extend a compliment about their work to their supervisor, volunteer to do office work at a local nonprofit agency, share your talents, gifts, and abilities by teaching a class.

Other activities:

_____

_____

Tech Sabbath Habit Plan: Week 12

This week, my tech-free day is (circle one):

Mon   Tues   Wed   Thurs   Fri   Sat   Sun

This week's encouraging thought: You can't enjoy today if you're worrying about tomorrow.

This week's technology challenge: Don't allow technology to steal your rest. Getting the proper amount of rest and sleep is important to the health of your body, mind, and soul. Getting less rest and sleep than normal is not good and can result in health-related issues. Seven to eight hours a night is necessary for your body to function properly each day.

Taking action: This week, get to bed early enough to ensure you get the recommended seven to eight hours of sleep. When we get plenty of rest, our energy is renewed, and our bodies, minds, and souls are refreshed and ready to tackle the day.

As you progress throughout the week, record the time you spent with technology and without it.

Bryan Brooks

Day	Date	Awake Time	Sleep Time	Technology Time		Tech-Free Time	
				Hours	Minutes	Hours	Minutes
		16 Hours	8 Hours				
		16 Hours	8 Hours				
		16 Hours	8 Hours				
		16 Hours	8 Hours				
		16 Hours	8 Hours				
		16 Hours	8 Hours				
		16 Hours	8 Hours				
Totals		112 Hours	56 Hours				

Transforming Activities

Activity ideas: Take a picnic lunch, get in your car and see where the day takes you, curl up with small book that you can read in an hour. Drink coffee in the morning sunshine. Get some water guns and have a water fight, sleep in a tree house, spend some quality time with a hammock. Hold the door for someone, extend a compliment about a job well done, send someone a handwritten note of thanks, treat a coworker to lunch for no reason. Make birthday cards for the elderly, run or walk in a charity race with friends, stage a carnival to promote community spirit.

Other activities:

_____

_____

Tech Sabbath Habit Plan: Week 13

This week, my tech-free day is (circle one):

Mon Tues Wed Thurs Fri Sat Sun

This week's encouraging thought: You can spend your time, waste your time, or invest your time. It's your choice.

This week's technology challenge: Reduce the amount of time you spend texting. The need to text has permeated our culture. It's impossible not to find someone texting, whether it's for fun or work. Texting is a popular way to communicate, but many of us use it as our only means of communication with friends, family, and coworkers. If you get the urge to text, call or go see that person and spend time with them instead. They will appreciate the fact that you set aside time out of your day to have a chat face-to-face.

Taking action: This week, reduce the amount of time you spend texting to no more than one hour a day.

As you progress throughout the week, record the time you spent with technology and without it.

Bryan Brooks

Day	Date	Awake Time	Sleep Time	Technology Time		Tech-Free Time	
				Hours	Minutes	Hours	Minutes
		16 Hours	8 Hours				
		16 Hours	8 Hours				
		16 Hours	8 Hours				
		16 Hours	8 Hours				
		16 Hours	8 Hours				
		16 Hours	8 Hours				
		16 Hours	8 Hours				
Totals		112 Hours	56 Hours				

Transforming Activities

Activity Ideas: Pick a favorite place to watch the sunset or sunrise and go there often, read all night and sleep all day, read the newspaper at a park. Play table tennis, skateboard, bathe in the ocean. Bring someone a cup of coffee without them asking; leave a flower on someone's desk; leave a nice, handwritten note for a coworker; help someone carry their stuff; pass out candy in the hallways; practice random acts of kindness; stage a marathon to raise money for a cause; volunteer your talents to help at charity auctions.

Other activities:

_____

_____

Tech Sabbath Habit Plan: Week 14

This week, my tech-free day is (circle one):

Mon   Tues   Wed   Thurs   Fri   Sat   Sun

This week's encouraging thought: Be kind to and love people whenever possible. Remember it's always possible.

This week's technology challenge: Avoid online viewing of inappropriate material. The Internet is saturated with such things as alcohol, gambling, pornography, drugs, hate/discrimination. It has become a toxic dump filled with bad and deceiving information. A good test for this is to ask yourself if your spouse, family, or accountability partner would approve of what you are doing. Scripture directs us to guard our hearts, for it determines the course of our lives.

Taking action: This week, do not view any inappropriate material online. Disconnect the Internet cable, and ask a family member or close friend to keep you accountable.

As you progress throughout the week, record the time you spent with technology and without it.

Day	Date	Awake Time	Sleep Time	Technology Time		Tech-Free Time	
				Hours	Minutes	Hours	Minutes
		16 Hours	8 Hours				
		16 Hours	8 Hours				
		16 Hours	8 Hours				
		16 Hours	8 Hours				
		16 Hours	8 Hours				
		16 Hours	8 Hours				
		16 Hours	8 Hours				
Totals		112 Hours	56 Hours				

Transforming Activities

Activity ideas: Escape to a bed and breakfast, plan a vacation to your favorite amusement park in the next six months. Find a peaceful piece of countryside and stay there for a while. Swim at the pool or in a lake or a river, play badminton. Allow a coworker's child to shadow you for a day and learn about your job, share positive news and quotes with others, take a photo of your colleagues at work and give it to them so their families can see them on the job, help an overworked colleague with some tasks. Take time to make sure your friends know that you appreciate them and that you're thankful for them, organize a coat drive in which old coats are donated for use by needy people. Share a smile and cheer someone up.

Other activities:

_____

_____

Tech Sabbath Habit Plan: Week 15

This week, my tech-free day is (circle one):

Mon Tues Wed Thurs Fri Sat Sun

This week's encouraging thought: If you see someone without a smile, give them one of yours.

This week's technology challenge: Don't let technology devices distract you in the car. Nearly 80 percent of American drivers admit to DWD (driving while distracted), and many of the distracted drivers admit to talking on cell phones, as well as checking and sending e-mail and instant messages while driving.[26] Pay attention to the road when you are driving, not technology devices. If you absolutely have to take a call, find a safe place to pull over so you can take the call, respond to a text message, plug in an address into your GPS device, etc.

Taking action: This week, do not allow any technology device in the car distract you. Turn the device off and put it away until you have arrived at your destination or you are stopped and parked in a place where you can safely use it.

As you progress throughout the week, record the time you spent with technology and without it.

Bryan Brooks

Day	Date	Awake Time	Sleep Time	Technology Time		Tech-Free Time	
				Hours	Minutes	Hours	Minutes
		16 Hours	8 Hours				
		16 Hours	8 Hours				
		16 Hours	8 Hours				
		16 Hours	8 Hours				
		16 Hours	8 Hours				
		16 Hours	8 Hours				
		16 Hours	8 Hours				
Totals		112 Hours	56 Hours				

Transforming Activities

Activity ideas: Rent a houseboat for a week, go jet skiing and/ or sailing. Go outside and lie on the grass, take a walk in the rain, sleep under the stars. Cheer up a sick friend with a visit or phone call, donate old eyeglasses to an organization or place that recycles them for the needy, collect old stuffed animals and dolls and donate them, help cook or serve a meal at a homeless shelter.

Other activities:

_____

_____

Tech Sabbath Habit Plan: Week 16

This week, my tech-free day is (circle one):

Mon Tues Wed Thurs Fri Sat Sun

This week's encouraging thought: Never let someone else choose your attitude or determine your level of joy and happiness.

This week's technology challenge: Do not hide behind your technology when communicating lengthy messages. Hiding behind technology is an easy thing to do and is becoming the norm when it comes to communicating lengthy messages. We all know or have experienced trying to communicate a lengthy message through e-mail, instant message, or multiple text messages using the proper tone, with sincerity and being careful with our words. This only goes so far and is usually still misinterpreted on the receiving party's end. E-mail discussion threads are a perfect example of this. How many times does an e-mail thread need to go back and forth before it's time to just pick up the phone? At some point, you just need to step away from the technology and personally communicate. Face-to-face interaction is good and healthy.

Taking action: This week, do not use technology to communicate lengthy messages. If your message is longer than one or two sentences, you need to pick up the phone or meet with that person and communicate with them face-to-face. You will gain respect and trust, and you will find yourself rediscovering the powerful art of communicating.

As you progress throughout the week, record the time you spent with technology and without it.

Day	Date	Awake Time	Sleep Time	Technology Time		Tech-Free Time	
				Hours	Minutes	Hours	Minutes
		16 Hours	8 Hours				
		16 Hours	8 Hours				
		16 Hours	8 Hours				
		16 Hours	8 Hours				
		16 Hours	8 Hours				
		16 Hours	8 Hours				
		16 Hours	8 Hours				
Totals		112 Hours	56 Hours				

Transforming Activities

Activity ideas: Tell your children why you love them, pat someone on the back, write a thank you note to a mentor or someone who has influenced your life in a positive way, give another driver your parking spot. Give free car washes, give toys to the children at the shelter or safe house, and give a bag of groceries to a homeless person. During National Nutrition Month in March, organize a nutrition awareness campaign, organize a food scavenger hunt to collect food for the needy, donate clothes to the needy.

Other activities:

_____

_____

Tech Sabbath Habit Plan: Week 17

This week, my tech-free day is (circle one):

Mon Tues Wed Thurs Fri Sat Sun

This week's encouraging thought: Your past mistakes are good preparation for a great future.

This week's technology challenge: Limit your video and computer-gaming time. Video and computer games can be a huge drain on your time. Recent surveys reveal that kids ages six to eleven consume more than twenty-eight viewing hours per week with all of their technology toys (TV, DVR, Internet, smart phone, portable game device, home game system, etc.).

Taking action: This week, set a time limit on your video and computer games to no more than one hour each day. Set a timer; it will help you stay on track. If necessary, find a friend or family member to hold you accountable to not going over your time limit.

As you progress throughout the week, record the time you spent with technology and without it.

Day	Date	Awake Time	Sleep Time	Technology Time		Tech-Free Time	
				Hours	Minutes	Hours	Minutes
		16 Hours	8 Hours				
		16 Hours	8 Hours				
		16 Hours	8 Hours				
		16 Hours	8 Hours				
		16 Hours	8 Hours				
		16 Hours	8 Hours				
		16 Hours	8 Hours				
Totals		112 Hours	56 Hours				

Transforming Activities

Activity ideas: Include a note or joke in your spouse's lunch. After reading a book you enjoyed, send a note of appreciation to the author. Exercise at least twice a week. Be a better listener, write a poem, learn about your family tree, build a tree house, and do some indoor rock climbing. Make "I care" kits with combs, toothbrushes, shampoo, etc., for homeless people. Bake bread on National Bread Day in November and deliver to the hungry, homeless, or just your neighbors. Help with repairs at a local homeless shelter.

Other activities:

_____

_____

Tech Sabbath Habit Plan: Week 18

This week, my tech-free day is (circle one):

Mon Tues Wed Thurs Fri Sat Sun

This week's encouraging thought: Change is the essence of life. Be willing to surrender what you are for what you could become.

This week's technology challenge: Don't bring technology on short trips. For convenience, portability, or whatever other reasons we concoct, there are times when leaving the technology at home is not a bad idea, and it will not hurt you or your lifestyle. Whether it is a quick trip to the grocery store to pick up the kids from school or going to get gas at the gas station, take advantage of the opportunity to not be connected.

Taking action: this week, leave the technology at home when going on short trips.

As you progress throughout the week, record the time you spent with technology and without it.

Bryan Brooks

Day	Date	Awake Time	Sleep Time	Technology Time		Tech-Free Time	
				Hours	Minutes	Hours	Minutes
		16 Hours	8 Hours				
		16 Hours	8 Hours				
		16 Hours	8 Hours				
		16 Hours	8 Hours				
		16 Hours	8 Hours				
		16 Hours	8 Hours				
		16 Hours	8 Hours				
Totals		112 Hours	56 Hours				

Transforming Activities

Activity ideas: Take your family or spouse on their dream vacation; visit as many of the fifty states as possible; take a pottery class; go see *Phantom of the Opera* live; attend at least one major sporting event; donate art supplies to kids in a homeless shelter; make a care package with mittens, socks, T-shirts, etc., for a child at a homeless shelter; start a program to help less fortunate people build their own houses.

Other activities:

_____

_____

Tech Sabbath Habit Plan: Week 19

This week, my tech-free day is (circle one):

Mon Tues Wed Thurs Fri Sat Sun

This week's encouraging thought: Strive for integrity—that means knowing your values in life and behaving in a way that is consistent with these values.

This week's technology challenge: Avoid wearing in- or on-ear devices (headphones, earbuds, Bluetooth-type headsets, etc.) while holding a conversation with people. These devices are all social cues that tell people you don't want to be disturbed or bothered.

Taking action: This week, do not wear in- or on-ear devices while conversing with friends, family, or coworkers. Show people you care by respecting how it makes others feel by not wearing any in- or on-ear devices when having a conversation with them.

As you progress throughout the week, record the time you spent with technology and without it.

Bryan Brooks

Day	Date	Awake Time	Sleep Time	Technology Time		Tech-Free Time	
				Hours	Minutes	Hours	Minutes
		16 Hours	8 Hours				
		16 Hours	8 Hours				
		16 Hours	8 Hours				
		16 Hours	8 Hours				
		16 Hours	8 Hours				
		16 Hours	8 Hours				
		16 Hours	8 Hours				
Totals		112 Hours	56 Hours				

Transforming Activities

Activity ideas: Make homemade ice cream or visit an ice cream parlor; share prayer requests that affect and concern the whole family, then pray about them; ask your children about their greatest fear and talk about it. Make popcorn, maybe even caramel corn. Take homeless children on outings, make first-aid kits for homeless shelters, contact a homeless shelter in your community and see if they already have a reading center and need help to keep the project going.

Other activities:

_____

_____

Tech Sabbath Habit Plan: Week 20

This week, my tech-free day is (circle one):

Mon Tues Wed Thurs Fri Sat Sun

This week's encouraging thought: To the world, you may be one person, but to one person, you may be the world!

This week's technology challenge: Don't let your technology use be a distraction to others. Focus on the people in your presence; they are more important than anything else. By your actions, show them that you are present physically and mentally.

Taking action: This week, make a point to not get distracted by technology when you interact with people. Turn it off, set it down, or put it away.

As you progress throughout the week, record the time you spent with technology and without it.

Bryan Brooks

Day	Date	Awake Time	Sleep Time	Technology Time		Tech-Free Time	
				Hours	Minutes	Hours	Minutes
		16 Hours	8 Hours				
		16 Hours	8 Hours				
		16 Hours	8 Hours				
		16 Hours	8 Hours				
		16 Hours	8 Hours				
		16 Hours	8 Hours				
		16 Hours	8 Hours				
Totals		112 Hours	56 Hours				

Transforming Activities

Activity ideas: Say, "I love you" when they *least* expect it, request a special song for him or her on the radio, plan an evening out for just the two of you, acknowledge the things your partner does for you. Set up a Saturday reading hour where you visit a homeless shelter once a month, bringing books to share and leave behind; collect items to deliver to homeless shelters (blankets, sheets, towels, toys, books, disposable diapers.)

Other activities:

_____

_____

Tech Sabbath Habit Plan: Week 21

This week, my tech-free day is (circle one):

Mon Tues Wed Thurs Fri Sat Sun

This week's encouraging thought: Instead of giving yourself reasons why you can't, give yourself reasons why you can.

This week's technology challenge: Don't look up information using your technology device while a discussion or argument is in progress with a friend, family member, or your spouse. Because of the ease and convenience of technology devices, they can quickly give us instant access to information. Using your technology device to prove your point or get an answer to resolve a disagreement and then jumping back into the conversation with the details is inconsiderate and typically will only make the matter worse.

Taking action: When you are in a discussion or argument with another person, don't look up information using your technology device. Take the time to discuss the matter through, and, if it is necessary at a later time and the other person is interested in your information, feel free to share the information you gathered.

As you progress throughout the week, record the time you spent with technology and without it.

Bryan Brooks

Day	Date	Awake Time	Sleep Time	Technology Time		Tech-Free Time	
				Hours	Minutes	Hours	Minutes
		16 Hours	8 Hours				
		16 Hours	8 Hours				
		16 Hours	8 Hours				
		16 Hours	8 Hours				
		16 Hours	8 Hours				
		16 Hours	8 Hours				
		16 Hours	8 Hours				
Totals		112 Hours	56 Hours				

Transforming Activities

Activity ideas: Play backgammon, spend quality time with a significant other in your life, play a board game together. Have a campout in your backyard, do your chores without being asked, spend time with your friends. Help neighbors paint and repair their homes, arrange for the local health department to conduct neighborhood health checks, volunteer to teach classes.

Other activities:

_____

_____

Tech Sabbath Habit Plan: Week 22

This week, my tech-free day is (circle one):

Mon Tues Wed Thurs Fri Sat Sun

This week's encouraging thought: Hope sees the invisible, feels the intangible, and achieves the impossible.

This week's technology challenge: Reduce your mobile technology footprint. Without realizing it, we can easily get ourselves swimming in a multitude of mobile technology devices.

Taking action: This week, take inventory and eliminate unnecessary mobile technology devices you have, such as mobile phones, smart phones, MP3 players, mobile DVD players, game players, or notebook computer systems. Donate them to a charity or nonprofit organization or dispose of them properly if they are beyond repair.

As you progress throughout the week, record the time you spent with technology and without it.

Day	Date	Awake Time	Sleep Time	Technology Time		Tech-Free Time	
				Hours	Minutes	Hours	Minutes
		16 Hours	8 Hours				
		16 Hours	8 Hours				
		16 Hours	8 Hours				
		16 Hours	8 Hours				
		16 Hours	8 Hours				
		16 Hours	8 Hours				
		16 Hours	8 Hours				
Totals		112 Hours	56 Hours				

Transforming Activities

Activity ideas: Take the highway, drive as far as you can, and see where you end up; hug a friend; say something nice to everyone you meet today. Take a trip to the local hobby store, collect some seashells at the beach, and try a new foreign food. Contact Habitat for Humanity to see how you can support them in your community, work with the local health department to set up an immunization day or clinic to immunize children against childhood diseases, organize a newcomers group in your neighborhood to welcome new families.

Other activities:

_____

_____

Tech Sabbath Habit Plan: Week 23

This week, my tech-free day is (circle one):

Mon Tues Wed Thurs Fri Sat Sun

This week's encouraging thought: Never give up on what you really want to do. The person with big dreams is more powerful than one with all the facts.

This week's technology challenge: Set down the technology and spend time with your family, friends, or your favorite hobby. Countless studies report that face-to-face family time is eroding as a result of increased levels of technology use.

Taking action: This week, do not allow any technology service or device become a more powerful draw than spending time with family, friends, other favorite activities, or hobbies that don't involve technology.

As you progress throughout the week, record the time you spent with technology and without it.

Bryan Brooks

Day	Date	Awake Time	Sleep Time	Technology Time		Tech-Free Time	
				Hours	Minutes	Hours	Minutes
		16 Hours	8 Hours				
		16 Hours	8 Hours				
		16 Hours	8 Hours				
		16 Hours	8 Hours				
		16 Hours	8 Hours				
		16 Hours	8 Hours				
		16 Hours	8 Hours				
Totals		112 Hours	56 Hours				

Transforming Activities

Activity ideas: Have a weekend away with close friends, take a gourmet cooking class, take a tour of Israel and the Holy Land. Ride a rollercoaster, play a game of pool, learn something new. Produce a neighborhood newspaper. Train to become a guide for your local tourist bureau. Volunteer to clean up trash at a community event or county fair.

Other activities:

_____

_____

Tech Sabbath Habit Plan: Week 24

This week, my tech-free day is (circle one):

Mon Tues Wed Thurs Fri Sat Sun

This week's encouraging thought: Positive attitudes create a chain reaction of positive thoughts.

This week's technology challenge: Institute a twenty-four-hour response time policy. Responding to every phone call and e-mail you receive creates constant interruption, disruption, and chaos. Not all e-mails and phone calls require an immediate response and action. By promptly responding to e-mail and phone calls all the time, you give people the impression that, whatever you are doing and wherever you are, you can be interrupted.

Taking action: This week, institute a twenty-four-hour response time policy for returning personal e-mails and phone calls.

As you progress throughout the week, record the time you spent with technology and without it.

Bryan Brooks

Day	Date	Awake Time	Sleep Time	Technology Time		Tech-Free Time	
				Hours	Minutes	Hours	Minutes
		16 Hours	8 Hours				
		16 Hours	8 Hours				
		16 Hours	8 Hours				
		16 Hours	8 Hours				
		16 Hours	8 Hours				
		16 Hours	8 Hours				
		16 Hours	8 Hours				
Totals		112 Hours	56 Hours				

Transforming Activities

Activity ideas: Get a blanket and a book and find a place to park it, get a therapeutic massage, give shoulder massages. Watch the clouds drift by, create your own comic strip, wear your pajamas all day. Make signs to label community buildings and sites of interest. Set up an art exhibit at a local business, school, or nursing home; volunteer to help clean out storm drains in your neighborhood.

Other activities:

_____

_____

Tech Sabbath Habit Plan: Week 25

This week, my tech-free day is (circle one):

Mon Tues Wed Thurs Fri Sat Sun

This week's encouraging thought: God gives us dreams a size too big so that we can grow in them.

This week's technology challenge: Avoid the urge to use technology on vacation. Instead, take the time to relax; it is a time to rejuvenate and refresh yourself, not quickly hop online, check your smart phone, and respond to e-mails from your laptop. Set an out-of-office agent in your e-mail communicating when you're on vacation and commit to not checking it. Your friends, family, and close relatives will all appreciate it, and you actually may create a new level of respect and, without realizing it, create positive changes in their lives.

Taking action: This week, avoid the urge to check e-mail or get online when on vacation.

As you progress throughout the week, record the time you spent with technology and without it.

Bryan Brooks

Day	Date	Awake Time	Sleep Time	Technology Time		Tech-Free Time	
				Hours	Minutes	Hours	Minutes
		16 Hours	8 Hours				
		16 Hours	8 Hours				
		16 Hours	8 Hours				
		16 Hours	8 Hours				
		16 Hours	8 Hours				
		16 Hours	8 Hours				
		16 Hours	8 Hours				
Totals		112 Hours	56 Hours				

Transforming Activities

Activity ideas: Get passionate about a cause and spend time helping it. Instead of just thinking about it, spend three months getting your body into optimum shape; look into your child's eyes, see yourself, and smile; go on a date every week with your spouse and kids. Organize a community chorus, orchestra, or band; volunteer to help set up for a community event; distribute leaf bags during the fall, encouraging residents to clean leaves from their streets and yards.

Other activities:

_____

_____

Tech Sabbath Habit Plan: Week 26

This week, my tech-free day is (circle one):

Mon Tues Wed Thurs Fri Sat Sun

This week's encouraging thought: Live well, laugh often, and love with all of your heart!

This week's technology challenge: Gain control of your e-mail. Answer or compose work and personal e-mails no more than three times a day. The morning, mid-afternoon, and early evening is more than enough opportunity to catch up on your e-mails and respond to them. By limiting yourself to checking e-mail no more than three times a day, you are establishing boundaries and letting people know who regularly send you e-mail that if a more urgent response is required, they must call you and discuss the matter or patiently wait for a response.

Taking action: This week, ignore the urge to check e-mails on your computer or smart phone consistently throughout the day. Limit it to three times a day: morning, mid-afternoon, and toward the end of the day (early evening).

As you progress throughout the week, record the time you spent with technology and without it.

Day	Date	Awake Time	Sleep Time	Technology Time		Tech-Free Time	
				Hours	Minutes	Hours	Minutes
		16 Hours	8 Hours				
		16 Hours	8 Hours				
		16 Hours	8 Hours				
		16 Hours	8 Hours				
		16 Hours	8 Hours				
		16 Hours	8 Hours				
		16 Hours	8 Hours				
Totals		112 Hours	56 Hours				

Transforming Activities

Activity ideas: Play a game of Scrabble, have a garage sale, go to an afternoon baseball game or a sport that you have never seen before. Go to an amusement park, the beach with sandwiches, adopt a billboard and use it for a public service announcement, campaign for additional lighting along poorly lighted streets, clean up vacant lots, collect supplies for persons who have been in a fire or natural disaster, help fix a rundown playground.

Other activities:

_____

_____

Tech Sabbath Habit Plan: Week 27

This week, my tech-free day is (circle one):

Mon Tues Wed Thurs Fri Sat Sun

This week's encouraging thought: Life isn't measured by the number of breaths we take, but by the moments that take our breath!

This week's technology challenge: Don't buy new technology without waiting twenty-four to forty-eight hours. We all get excited from time to time when we see technology advertisements that get our blood pumping. This euphoria is what influences our decision to buy a particular technology product or service. It's okay to wait. Waiting will defer those things we want versus what we need.

Taking action: This week, do not purchase any technology without first sleeping on it for a period of twenty-four to forty-eight hours.

As you progress throughout the week, record the time you spent with technology and without it.

Day	Date	Awake Time	Sleep Time	Technology Time		Tech-Free Time	
				Hours	Minutes	Hours	Minutes
		16 Hours	8 Hours				
		16 Hours	8 Hours				
		16 Hours	8 Hours				
		16 Hours	8 Hours				
		16 Hours	8 Hours				
		16 Hours	8 Hours				
		16 Hours	8 Hours				
Totals		112 Hours	56 Hours				

Transforming Activities

Activity ideas: Plan a journey somewhere, go to a flea market, lounge on a hammock. Go to a hockey game or a theater play or run through your garden sprinkler. Start a yard of the week award for your neighborhood, support a local parade by participating in it, spruce up and paint the community or youth center, plant a community garden. Adopt a town monument and keep it clean.

Other activities:

_____

_____

Tech Sabbath Habit Plan: Week 28

This week, my tech-free day is (circle one):

Mon Tues Wed Thurs Fri Sat Sun

This week's encouraging thought: The love of a family is life's greatest blessing.

This week's technology challenge: Don't waste your time in chat rooms. Chat rooms are Internet environments where you can use text to have real-time conversations with many people at the same time. Some chat rooms use text-based conversation threads, while others create environments where visitors can represent themselves using avatars (or characters). Chat rooms are huge time-wasters.

Taking action: This week, do not visit chat rooms of any kind. Chat room discussions may become sexual or violent, or they may promote hate against others.

As you progress throughout the week, record the time you spent with technology and without it.

Day	Date	Awake Time	Sleep Time	Technology Time		Tech-Free Time	
				Hours	Minutes	Hours	Minutes
		16 Hours	8 Hours				
		16 Hours	8 Hours				
		16 Hours	8 Hours				
		16 Hours	8 Hours				
		16 Hours	8 Hours				
		16 Hours	8 Hours				
		16 Hours	8 Hours				
Totals		112 Hours	56 Hours				

Transforming Activities

Activity ideas: On a hot day, get a kiddy wading pool, fill it up, then sit in it for most of the afternoon. Play backgammon outdoors somewhere. Go to an art museum, start a pillow fight, visit a farm. Clean an elderly neighbor's driveway and sidewalk, clean up after a natural disaster, organize a local blood drive with the American Red Cross.

Other activities:

_____

_____

Tech Sabbath Habit Plan: Week 29

This week, my tech-free day is (circle one):

Mon   Tues   Wed   Thurs   Fri   Sat   Sun

This week's encouraging thought: Good habits are formed; bad habits we fall into.

This week's technology challenge: Take time to reboot yourself. It is important to do this at least three times a day. Breathe in slowly and deeply, hold it for a few seconds, and exhale slowly. Concentrating on breathing a few times each day forces you to calm down.

Taking action: This week, take five to ten minutes every hour during the day to breathe deeply and slowly.

As you progress throughout the week, record the time you spent with technology and without it.

Day	Date	Awake Time	Sleep Time	Technology Time		Tech-Free Time	
				Hours	Minutes	Hours	Minutes
		16 Hours	8 Hours				
		16 Hours	8 Hours				
		16 Hours	8 Hours				
		16 Hours	8 Hours				
		16 Hours	8 Hours				
		16 Hours	8 Hours				
		16 Hours	8 Hours				
Totals		112 Hours	56 Hours				

Transforming Activities

Activity ideas: See the Olympics, shower in a waterfall, snorkel, take a hot air balloon ride, take an RV trip. Go camping on the beach; go to your nearest trampoline and bounce; organize a campaign to raise money to buy and install new playground equipment for a park; survey community agencies to learn the leading causes of accidents in your community, then design a campaign to reduce accidents; paint a mural or clean up a local park; take care of yard work for neighbors who are away on vacation.

Other activities:

_____

_____

Tech Sabbath Habit Plan: Week 30

This week, my tech-free day is (circle one):

Mon Tues Wed Thurs Fri Sat Sun

This week's encouraging thought: If you look for the positive things in life, you will find them.

This week's technology challenge: Stop using technology when you are asked to stop. A sign that your technology use is getting out of control is when your family, close relatives, coworkers, or friends ask you to stop using it for a specific reason, but you refuse to do so.

Taking action: This week, stop using technology when you are asked to stop.

As you progress throughout the week, record the time you spent with technology and without it.

Bryan Brooks

Day	Date	Awake Time	Sleep Time	Technology Time		Tech-Free Time	
				Hours	Minutes	Hours	Minutes
		16 Hours	8 Hours				
		16 Hours	8 Hours				
		16 Hours	8 Hours				
		16 Hours	8 Hours				
		16 Hours	8 Hours				
		16 Hours	8 Hours				
		16 Hours	8 Hours				
Totals		112 Hours	56 Hours				

Transforming Activities

Activity ideas: Go see a symphony; fill your tank with gas and drive till it's half gone and come back; go to the yellow pages and pick the seventh restaurant, eat the seventh entrée, and order the seventh dessert. Go roller-skating, sing karaoke, visit a bee-keeper. Read aloud to a person who is visually impaired, build park benches, help winterize homes in a poverty-stricken neighborhood, lend a helping hand at a local community center, conduct a neighborhood drive to collect used furniture.

Other activities:

_____

_____

Tech Sabbath Habit Plan: Week 31

This week, my tech-free day is (circle one):

Mon Tues Wed Thurs Fri Sat Sun

This week's encouraging thought: You are today where your thoughts have brought you; you will be tomorrow where your thoughts take you.

This week's technology challenge: When using your smart phone or cell phone in public places, on buses, or in waiting rooms, do not use your speakerphone! It is inconsiderate to openly share your personal conversation details with everyone out loud. Also, no one has any interest in listening to it.

Taking action: This week, be respectful of others and avoid using the speakerphone on your smart phone/cell phone in public places, on buses, or in waiting rooms.

As you progress throughout the week, record the time you spent with technology and without it.

Day	Date	Awake Time	Sleep Time	Technology Time		Tech-Free Time	
				Hours	Minutes	Hours	Minutes
		16 Hours	8 Hours				
		16 Hours	8 Hours				
		16 Hours	8 Hours				
		16 Hours	8 Hours				
		16 Hours	8 Hours				
		16 Hours	8 Hours				
		16 Hours	8 Hours				
Totals		112 Hours	56 Hours				

Transforming Activities

Activity ideas: Visit the library and take out books or take advantage of some of their great programs; go canoeing or kayaking. Ride a scooter, read, sell lemonade, go rollerblading. Refrain from negative talk, concentrate on the positive, show your appreciation to coworkers through words and notes. Extend a hand to someone in need. Give your full attention and listen, pay a compliment at least once a day, say something nice to everyone you meet today.

Other activities:

_____

_____

Tech Sabbath Habit Plan: Week 32

This week, my tech-free day is (circle one):

Mon Tues Wed Thurs Fri Sat Sun

This week's encouraging thought: Think highly of yourself, for the world takes you at your own estimate.

This week's technology challenge: Avoid the urge to online shop unless purchasing a specific budgeted item. Most people don't think twice about getting new technology. They buy it, and then it becomes embedded in their life with little value added. Avoid the temptation. Ask yourself questions before you purchase: *Do I really need this? How is this going to help me? What purpose is this going to play in my life?*

Taking action: This week, avoid the urge to online shop for technology items unless purchasing a specific budgeted item.

As you progress throughout the week, record the time you spent with technology and without it.

Day	Date	Awake Time	Sleep Time	Technology Time		Tech-Free Time	
				Hours	Minutes	Hours	Minutes
		16 Hours	8 Hours				
		16 Hours	8 Hours				
		16 Hours	8 Hours				
		16 Hours	8 Hours				
		16 Hours	8 Hours				
		16 Hours	8 Hours				
		16 Hours	8 Hours				
Totals		112 Hours	56 Hours				

Transforming Activities

Activity ideas: Stroll through a public garden or work on your own garden. Make a chalk mural in your driveway, make a birdhouse, and join a book club at the library, Borders, or Barnes & Noble. Offer to help out with the not-so-pleasant tasks at work; write a letter commending an employee who helped you. Do some yard work for a person who is ill, start a collection drive for old sports equipment and donate it to families.

Other activities:

_____

_____

Tech Sabbath Habit Plan: Week 33

This week, my tech-free day is (circle one):

Mon Tues Wed Thurs Fri Sat Sun

This week's encouraging thought: Learn from yesterday, live for today, hope for tomorrow.

This week's technology challenge: Cut back on technology services that are truly unnecessary. Yes, there is a convenience factor that comes from most technology services, and you may feel that most of them are necessity, but they are not—for example, having over three hundred channels on your digital cable box, two hundred channels on your satellite radio, a DVD and game rental subscription, and a cell phone plan that has all the bells and whistles. It all adds up to overspending and overindulging. Take the time to clean your technology house. You will not only discover you save money and time, but you will end up less distracted and more satisfied by having technology services that better fit your specific needs.

Taking action: This week, evaluate and eliminate all technology services that you subscribe to and cut back on ones that are truly unnecessary.

As you progress throughout the week, record the time you spent with technology and without it.

Bryan Brooks

Day	Date	Awake Time	Sleep Time	Technology Time		Tech-Free Time	
				Hours	Minutes	Hours	Minutes
		16 Hours	8 Hours				
		16 Hours	8 Hours				
		16 Hours	8 Hours				
		16 Hours	8 Hours				
		16 Hours	8 Hours				
		16 Hours	8 Hours				
		16 Hours	8 Hours				
Totals		112 Hours	56 Hours				

Transforming Activities

Activity ideas: Take a train ride, take a week vacation in your own hometown, take a weekend trip by yourself. Go whale watching, ride the ferryboat, build a model airplane. Plant a garden or tree where the whole neighborhood can enjoy it. Set up a recycling system for your home, and participate in your neighborhood curbside recycling pick up. Organize a carpooling campaign in your neighborhood to cut down on air pollution.

Other activities:

_____

_____

Tech Sabbath Habit Plan: Week 34

This week, my tech-free day is (circle one):

Mon Tues Wed Thurs Fri Sat Sun

This week's encouraging thought: When you go for the impossible, you make way for the incredible.

This week's technology challenge: Institute a three-times-a-day policy for listening to voice mail. In the morning, right around lunchtime, and in the evening are typical times for checking in and following up on voicemail messages. When you decide to listen to your voice mail messages every time one comes in, this becomes a major distraction to your day.

Taking action: This week, institute a policy of only listening to voice mail messages on your mobile phone or smart phone device no more than three times a day. In the morning, right around lunch, and in the evening are good times for checking voice mail.

As you progress throughout the week, record the time you spent with technology and without it.

Day	Date	Awake Time	Sleep Time	Technology Time		Tech-Free Time	
				Hours	Minutes	Hours	Minutes
		16 Hours	8 Hours				
		16 Hours	8 Hours				
		16 Hours	8 Hours				
		16 Hours	8 Hours				
		16 Hours	8 Hours				
		16 Hours	8 Hours				
		16 Hours	8 Hours				
Totals		112 Hours	56 Hours				

Transforming Activities

Activity ideas: Volunteer to be a tutor in a school, adopt a homeless pet from the Humane Society, volunteer to read to students in the classroom. Clean classrooms for a school custodian, sing at a nursing home, offer a couple of hours of babysitting to parents. Set up a seed or plant exchange in your neighborhood, grow fresh flowers and deliver them to someone to brighten their day, make birdfeeders for public places.

Other activities:

_____

_____

Tech Sabbath Habit Plan: Week 35

This week, my tech-free day is (circle one):

Mon Tues Wed Thurs Fri Sat Sun

This week's encouraging thought: Don't be afraid of the space between your dreams and reality. If you can dream it, you can make it so.

This week's technology challenge: Avoid allowing technology to become a commonplace of enjoyment. Too many times, without even realizing it, we turn to technology to bring us excitement, enjoyment, and happiness in our lives.

Taking action: This week, do not allow technology to become your place of enjoyment. Find other tech-free things to do.

As you progress throughout the week, record the time you spent with technology and without it.

Day	Date	Awake Time	Sleep Time	Technology Time		Tech-Free Time	
				Hours	Minutes	Hours	Minutes
		16 Hours	8 Hours				
		16 Hours	8 Hours				
		16 Hours	8 Hours				
		16 Hours	8 Hours				
		16 Hours	8 Hours				
		16 Hours	8 Hours				
		16 Hours	8 Hours				
Totals		112 Hours	56 Hours				

Transforming Activities

Activity ideas: Transport someone who can't drive, write a note to your kids and spouse and tell them why they are special, leave a treat or handmade note of thanks for a delivery person or mail carrier. Give toys to children at a shelter, laugh out loud often, and share your smile generously. Adopt an acre of a park or a mile of roadside to keep clean; elect a family energy watchdog to shut off lights, radios, and TVs when not in use; help everyone in your family conserve water; and clean up trash along a river or in a park.

Other activities:

_____

_____

Tech Sabbath Habit Plan: Week 36

This week, my tech-free day is (circle one):

Mon Tues Wed Thurs Fri Sat Sun

This week's encouraging thought: The key to happiness is having dreams. The key to success is making your dreams come true.

This week's technology challenge: Pay less attention to your technology and more attention to making life events a priority. Put more effort and attention toward involving yourself in family gatherings, graduation ceremonies, baby births, marriages, birthdays, etc. Enjoy life's precious moments; they only come once in a lifetime.

Taking action: This week, don't spend time with technology so much that you miss out on important life events. Get out from behind the computer, your smart phone, your video game system and live life!

As you progress throughout the week, record the time you spent with technology and without it.

Bryan Brooks

Day	Date	Awake Time	Sleep Time	Technology Time		Tech-Free Time	
				Hours	Minutes	Hours	Minutes
		16 Hours	8 Hours				
		16 Hours	8 Hours				
		16 Hours	8 Hours				
		16 Hours	8 Hours				
		16 Hours	8 Hours				
		16 Hours	8 Hours				
		16 Hours	8 Hours				
Totals		112 Hours	56 Hours				

Transforming Activities

Activity ideas: Spend the night at a bed and breakfast, take a cake- and cookie-decorating class, take a firehouse tour. Play charades, create paper snowflakes, create a photo collage. Have a thumb-wrestling match; have an arm-wrestling match. Create a habitat for wildlife, create a campaign to encourage biking and walking, test the health of the water in your local lakes, rivers, or streams.

Other activities:

_____

_____

Tech Sabbath Habit Plan: Week 37

This week, my tech-free day is (circle one):

Mon Tues Wed Thurs Fri Sat Sun

This week's encouraging thought: Never lose sight of the importance of your health, a beautiful sunrise, watching your kids sleep, or the smell of rain. It's often the little things that really matter in life.

This week's technology challenge: Invest your time wisely into things that matter. What you are doing with your time each day is either spent wisely or wasted away. One example is investing time and effort into your personal friendships and family relationships. It shows you deeply and truly care about them. When you truly begin to value your time, you'll find that you have more of it to do the things that matter.

Taking action: This week, make it a point to spend your time wisely on the things that are important. Set up a lunch date with a friend.

As you progress throughout the week, record the time you spent with technology and without it.

Day	Date	Awake Time	Sleep Time	Technology Time		Tech-Free Time	
				Hours	Minutes	Hours	Minutes
		16 Hours	8 Hours				
		16 Hours	8 Hours				
		16 Hours	8 Hours				
		16 Hours	8 Hours				
		16 Hours	8 Hours				
		16 Hours	8 Hours				
		16 Hours	8 Hours				
Totals		112 Hours	56 Hours				

Transforming Activities

Activity ideas: Play Marco Polo; play rock, paper, scissors; go window-shopping; go on a drive to an unfamiliar place that peaks your interest. Make your own colored clay, make a battery out of a potato, play Simon Says, go to a basketball court and play a game of Horse. Visit a nursing home, rake leaves, clean gutters, or wash windows for a senior citizen; pick up medicine for an elderly person.

Other activities:

_____

_____

Tech Sabbath Habit Plan: Week 38

This week, my tech-free day is (circle one):

Mon Tues Wed Thurs Fri Sat Sun

This week's encouraging thought: Some people succeed because they are destined to, but most people succeed because they are determined to.

This week's technology challenge: Limit your podcasting intake. There are a lot of great podcasts out there filled with information you need or should hear. Be careful not to become a podcast junkie—a person that has media pouring into their minds every minute of every day.

Taking action: This week, set a combined time limit when listening to podcasts to one hour a day. Set a timer to keep track of time.

As you progress throughout the week, record the time you spent with technology and without it.

Day	Date	Awake Time	Sleep Time	Technology Time		Tech-Free Time	
				Hours	Minutes	Hours	Minutes
		16 Hours	8 Hours				
		16 Hours	8 Hours				
		16 Hours	8 Hours				
		16 Hours	8 Hours				
		16 Hours	8 Hours				
		16 Hours	8 Hours				
		16 Hours	8 Hours				
Totals		112 Hours	56 Hours				

Transforming Activities

Activity ideas: Play Hangman, give your spouse a fifteen-minute scalp massage, offer to do a chore that he or she normally does, blow your loved one a kiss or give him or her a wink as you're walking out the door. Have a Mentos soda explosion, dig a hole, create a vinegar volcano, make a cardboard box fort. Pick up the morning paper for a senior neighbor on your way to school, form a mall patrol with your friends to help seniors with their shopping, form a kids carwash squad to clean and wash seniors' cars, write your grandfriend a letter or write letters for an elderly person.

Other activities:

_____

_____

Tech Sabbath Habit Plan: Week 39

This week, my tech-free day is (circle one):

Mon Tues Wed Thurs Fri Sat Sun

This week's encouraging thought: Every accomplishment starts with the decision to try.

This week's technology challenge: Don't allow your technology to create disorganization in your life. With so many different applications and features that are available today with the different devices and services to help organize our lives, technology easily can create serious disorganization. Keep it under control by using it in ways that help you stay organized. One example would be to use only one e-mail, calendar, and address book application on one device instead of multiple devices. Syncing this information between multiple devices can be chaotic, and if syncing doesn't occur as you expect it to, you will lose data and more than likely end up with pieces of information scattered between devices.

Taking action: This week, don't allow technology to make you late or miss important meetings, dates, or appointments.

As you progress throughout the week, record the time you spent with technology and without it.

Day	Date	Awake Time	Sleep Time	Technology Time		Tech-Free Time	
				Hours	Minutes	Hours	Minutes
		16 Hours	8 Hours				
		16 Hours	8 Hours				
		16 Hours	8 Hours				
		16 Hours	8 Hours				
		16 Hours	8 Hours				
		16 Hours	8 Hours				
		16 Hours	8 Hours				
Totals		112 Hours	56 Hours				

Transforming Activities

Activity ideas: Enjoy a concert in the park; visit a museum; write out ten things that make you happy, then do one of them. Dance, skateboard, or write. Go for a walk with a senior citizen in your community; with the help of family and friends, hold a summer-time dance party.

Other activities:

_____

_____

Tech Sabbath Habit Plan: Week 40

This week, my tech-free day is (circle one):

Mon Tues Wed Thurs Fri Sat Sun

This week's encouraging thought: Every success is built on the ability to do better than good enough.

This week's technology challenge: Reduce the amount of hardware-related technology tools you have. For example, four computer systems, three televisions, a game station, MP3 player, two stereo systems, two CD/DVD players, a satellite radio, a GPS, two digital cameras, and a video camcorder is too much. Take inventory and get rid of stuff.

Taking action: This week, work on reducing the amount of hardware-related technology tools you have in your life.

As you progress throughout the week, record the time you spent with technology and without it.

Bryan Brooks

Day	Date	Awake Time	Sleep Time	Technology Time		Tech-Free Time	
				Hours	Minutes	Hours	Minutes
		16 Hours	8 Hours				
		16 Hours	8 Hours				
		16 Hours	8 Hours				
		16 Hours	8 Hours				
		16 Hours	8 Hours				
		16 Hours	8 Hours				
		16 Hours	8 Hours				
Totals		112 Hours	56 Hours				

Transforming Activities

Activity ideas: Attend a local opera house, go to the carnival/state fair, sneak up to your spouse and kiss the back of his or her neck, work on home improvement projects together. Play Frisbee, go for a bike ride, play a sport of some kind (baseball, basketball, football, etc.). Deliver meals to homebound individuals, offer to pick up groceries with or for a senior citizen, help senior citizens in your neighborhood obtain and install locks or smoke alarms.

Other activities:

_____

_____

Tech Sabbath Habit Plan: Week 41

This week, my tech-free day is (circle one):

Mon Tues Wed Thurs Fri Sat Sun

This week's encouraging thought: Life is a continual process of remaking ourselves.

This week's technology challenge: Avoid looking at any inappropriate websites. This includes, pornography, mutilation, torture, horror, illegal, gambling, and recreational drug use or hate/discrimination websites.

Taking action: This week, do not look at inappropriate websites. Find something more productive to do.

As you progress throughout the week, record the time you spent with technology and without it.

Day	Date	Awake Time	Sleep Time	Technology Time		Tech-Free Time	
				Hours	Minutes	Hours	Minutes
		16 Hours	8 Hours				
		16 Hours	8 Hours				
		16 Hours	8 Hours				
		16 Hours	8 Hours				
		16 Hours	8 Hours				
		16 Hours	8 Hours				
		16 Hours	8 Hours				
Totals		112 Hours	56 Hours				

Transforming Activities

Activity ideas: Write down whatever comes into your head in a journal, surprise a friend that you haven't seen in a long time, eat your dinner on the beach or by a lake. Read some comic books. Take a pet to a nursing home, do art projects (like finger painting) with people in nursing homes. Organize a sing-a-long; offer to read to people in a nursing home.

Other activities:

_____

_____

Tech Sabbath Habit Plan: Week 42

This week, my tech-free day is (circle one):

Mon Tues Wed Thurs Fri Sat Sun

This week's encouraging thought: Always be yourself, because in the end, that's what people will remember about you.

This week's technology challenge: Avoid the temptation to follow technology trends. Technology changes rapidly, and as a result, there will always be new advancements being released. By avoiding following technology trends, you not only save yourself money but headaches as well.

Taking action: This week, avoid following technology trends. Feeling like you always need the latest and greatest technology devices and services is not only expensive but also wasteful for the environment, and it steals your time.

As you progress throughout the week, record the time you spent with technology and without it.

Day	Date	Awake Time	Sleep Time	Technology Time		Tech-Free Time	
				Hours	Minutes	Hours	Minutes
		16 Hours	8 Hours				
		16 Hours	8 Hours				
		16 Hours	8 Hours				
		16 Hours	8 Hours				
		16 Hours	8 Hours				
		16 Hours	8 Hours				
		16 Hours	8 Hours				
Totals		112 Hours	56 Hours				

Transforming Activities

Activity ideas: Feed the ducks at the park, spend the entire morning in bed, unplug the phone, and take a bubble bath. Ask a grandparent about their wedding day or some of their most favorite fun moments, go for a walk together, go help a charity for the day. Volunteer at an animal shelter. Help clean up, play with the animals, or do whatever is needed to make the shelter a nicer temporary home for the animals; find out about raising a dog for persons with disabilities; raise money for pet causes by organizing a pet photo session.

Other activities:

_____

_____

Tech Sabbath Habit Plan: Week 43

This week, my tech-free day is (circle one):

Mon Tues Wed Thurs Fri Sat Sun

This week's encouraging thought: Never give up on something that you can't go a day without thinking about.

This week's technology challenge: Unsubscribe to online newsletters that you have not looked at for twenty-four hours or more. Having your e-mail inbox filled with online newsletters clutters your life and creates more undue stress.

Taking action: This week, go through your e-mail and unsubscribe to online newsletters subscriptions that you have not looked at for twenty-four hours or more. Only keep those that you actively read.

As you progress throughout the week, record the time you spent with technology and without it.

Bryan Brooks

Day	Date	Awake Time	Sleep Time	Technology Time		Tech-Free Time	
				Hours	Minutes	Hours	Minutes
		16 Hours	8 Hours				
		16 Hours	8 Hours				
		16 Hours	8 Hours				
		16 Hours	8 Hours				
		16 Hours	8 Hours				
		16 Hours	8 Hours				
		16 Hours	8 Hours				
Totals		112 Hours	56 Hours				

Transforming Activities

Activity ideas: Take a nap, play cards, shop for a really cool book, learn a new word in the dictionary. Take advantage of local cultural events; swing on a tire swing. Organize a pet show for a local nursing home, and, with the support of a vet clinic, organize a campaign to get animals neutered and spayed at a reduced rate.

Other activities:

_____

_____

Tech Sabbath Habit Plan: Week 44

This week, my tech-free day is (circle one):

Mon Tues Wed Thurs Fri Sat Sun

This week's encouraging thought: Don't be ordinary. Be extraordinary.

This week's technology challenge: Reduce your involvement in online groups and forums. With the multitude of online groups and forums available online, it is easy to spend a lot of time participating in so many of them that it occupies excessive amounts of time.

Taking action: This week, reduce your involvement in online group and forums to those that are truly necessary and valuable. If there are any that you do not actively participate in on a daily or weekly basis, unsubscribe to them.

As you progress throughout the week, record the time you spent with technology and without it.

Bryan Brooks

Day	Date	Awake Time	Sleep Time	Technology Time		Tech-Free Time	
				Hours	Minutes	Hours	Minutes
		16 Hours	8 Hours				
		16 Hours	8 Hours				
		16 Hours	8 Hours				
		16 Hours	8 Hours				
		16 Hours	8 Hours				
		16 Hours	8 Hours				
		16 Hours	8 Hours				
Totals		112 Hours	56 Hours				

Transforming Activities

Activity ideas: Rest under your favorite tree, sit and think somewhere, have a barbeque and enjoy each other's conversation. Go to a waterslide, go to the playground, learn about and do pet therapy with your animal at nursing homes and daycare centers, form a "we love animals" club and volunteer to care for animals at a children's zoo, plan a special awareness event during Be Kind to Animals Week in May, organize a community dog wash.

Other activities:

_____

_____

Tech Sabbath Habit Plan: Week 45

This week, my tech-free day is (circle one):

Mon Tues Wed Thurs Fri Sat Sun

This week's encouraging thought: There is no greater treasure than the respect and love of a close friend.

This week's technology challenge: Eliminate the amount of RSS feeds to only those that you actively read. Really Simple Syndication feeds can be informative and keep you informed of things going on in the world; however, if you have too many, the information can be overwhelming and eat up your valuable time.

Taking action: This week, sort through and unsubscribe to RSS feeds that you don't actively read.

As you progress throughout the week, record the time you spent with technology and without it.

Day	Date	Awake Time	Sleep Time	Technology Time		Tech-Free Time	
				Hours	Minutes	Hours	Minutes
		16 Hours	8 Hours				
		16 Hours	8 Hours				
		16 Hours	8 Hours				
		16 Hours	8 Hours				
		16 Hours	8 Hours				
		16 Hours	8 Hours				
		16 Hours	8 Hours				
Totals		112 Hours	56 Hours				

Transforming Activities

Activity ideas: Learn a new water dive, learn to throw a boomerang, go to the beach and look for sand dollars and shells. Float down a slow river on a tube, get a random summer job, go boating. Volunteer to clean out animal shelters; collect and sort newspapers to donate to a local animal shelter; collect food and supplies needed for a local zoo, animal shelter, or food bank; adopt a zoo animal.

Other activities:

_____

_____

Tech Sabbath Habit Plan: Week 46

This week, my tech-free day is (circle one):

Mon Tues Wed Thurs Fri Sat Sun

This week's encouraging thought: Achievement is not the most important thing; authenticity is.

This week's technology challenge: Limit your blog writing and reading time. For those that may not know what blogs are, these are website-based on-going narratives written by one or more individuals about many different topics (i.e., your family vacation, work-related subjects, political opinions, personal testimonies, etc.). If you are a writer of blogs or a reader of them, you know how easy it is to spend several hours a day writing or reading them.

Taking action: This week, set a combined time limit to only write and read blogs no more than one hour a day. Set a timer to keep track of time.

As you progress throughout the week, record the time you spent with technology and without it.

Day	Date	Awake Time	Sleep Time	Technology Time		Tech-Free Time	
				Hours	Minutes	Hours	Minutes
		16 Hours	8 Hours				
		16 Hours	8 Hours				
		16 Hours	8 Hours				
		16 Hours	8 Hours				
		16 Hours	8 Hours				
		16 Hours	8 Hours				
		16 Hours	8 Hours				
Totals		112 Hours	56 Hours				

Transforming Activities

Activity ideas: Tell someone the story of your life, sparing no details; write down your personal mission statement, follow it, and revise it from time to time. See a lunar eclipse. Send a message in a bottle. Get to know your neighbors. Find homes in shelters for abandoned pets.

Other activities:

_____

_____

Tech Sabbath Habit Plan: Week 47

This week, my tech-free day is (circle one):

Mon Tues Wed Thurs Fri Sat Sun

This week's encouraging thought: Nothing in this world is impossible to a willing heart.

This week's technology challenge: Stay away from using technology when you're emotionally charged up or depressed. It is easy to find yourself turning to it at times when you are feeling uncomfortable, irritated, frustrated, sad, or moody. When this happens, you risk doing things you wouldn't normally do, like viewing inappropriate websites, sending hurtful emails, etc. Don't take the chance.

Taking action: This week, when feeling upset or moody, catch yourself and avoid turning to technology. By not turning to technology when you are feeling like this, you are less likely to take risky actions.

As you progress throughout the week, record the time you spent with technology and without it.

Day	Date	Awake Time	Sleep Time	Technology Time		Tech-Free Time	
				Hours	Minutes	Hours	Minutes
		16 Hours	8 Hours				
		16 Hours	8 Hours				
		16 Hours	8 Hours				
		16 Hours	8 Hours				
		16 Hours	8 Hours				
		16 Hours	8 Hours				
		16 Hours	8 Hours				
Totals		112 Hours	56 Hours				

Transforming Activities

Activity ideas: Coordinate and have a family reunion, make fridge magnets with your photos and give them to family members and close relatives, play Bingo, volunteer to help at a Special Olympics event, set up a buddy system for kids with special needs at your school, raise money for Braille or large print books for blind or visually impaired people.

Other activities:

_____

_____

Tech Sabbath Habit Plan: Week 48

This week, my tech-free day is (circle one):

Mon Tues Wed Thurs Fri Sat Sun

This week's encouraging thought: Humility is the ladder to divine understanding.

This week's technology challenge: Steer clear of peer-to-peer file sharing networking sites. This is not only a big time-waster, but the majority of the files on these sites are illegal and you risk getting your computer saturated by a multitude of computer infections.

Taking action: This week, do not use peer-to-peer file-sharing networking sites. In fact, if you have this kind of software installed, remove it. Examples of this kind of software would be: Limewire, Bit torrent, eMule, Ares, Morpheus.

As you progress throughout the week, record the time you spent with technology and without it.

Day	Date	Awake Time	Sleep Time	Technology Time		Tech-Free Time	
				Hours	Minutes	Hours	Minutes
		16 Hours	8 Hours				
		16 Hours	8 Hours				
		16 Hours	8 Hours				
		16 Hours	8 Hours				
		16 Hours	8 Hours				
		16 Hours	8 Hours				
		16 Hours	8 Hours				
Totals		112 Hours	56 Hours				

Transforming Activities

Activity ideas: Hang out with senior people—they have great stories and sometimes need the company. Decorate blank T-shirts, Make deep-fried Twinkies, clean out your closet, volunteer at an agency that works with children with disabilities, read books or the newspaper on tape for blind or visually impaired people.

Other activities:

_____

_____

Tech Sabbath Habit Plan: Week 49

This week, my tech-free day is (circle one):

Mon Tues Wed Thurs Fri Sat Sun

This week's encouraging thought: Successful people have the courage to take action where others hesitate.

This week's technology challenge: Limit your online computer game time. Playing online computer games can be quite the diversion and is an easy way to waste away a ton of your precious time. Competitiveness, accessibility, the intellectual challenge, or the abundance of game choices online are just a few of the many reasons people play online computer games. As a result of these reasons and many others, this can easily result in an obsessive addiction that could lead to major health problems and isolation.

Taking action: This week, set a combined time limit on the amount of personal time you play online computer games to no more than one hour a day. Set a timer to keep track of time.

As you progress throughout the week, record the time you spent with technology and without it.

Day	Date	Awake Time	Sleep Time	Technology Time		Tech-Free Time	
				Hours	Minutes	Hours	Minutes
		16 Hours	8 Hours				
		16 Hours	8 Hours				
		16 Hours	8 Hours				
		16 Hours	8 Hours				
		16 Hours	8 Hours				
		16 Hours	8 Hours				
		16 Hours	8 Hours				
Totals		112 Hours	56 Hours				

Transforming Activities

Activity ideas: Go prospecting for gold, go scuba diving, go see the local big sporting events. Swim with dolphins, catch a snow-flake with your tongue, take old-time photos of your family and friends. Prepare sack lunches and deliver them to homeless or homebound people, bring toys to children in the cancer ward of a hospital, work with physically challenged kids on an art project.

Other activities:

_____

_____

Tech Sabbath Habit Plan: Week 50

This week, my tech-free day is (circle one):

Mon Tues Wed Thurs Fri Sat Sun

This week's encouraging thought: Act as though you cannot fail but keep a humble spirit.

This week's technology challenge: Gradually start your day with technology and end your day unwinding from it. Immediately connecting yourself by reading e-mails or text messages or listening to voice mails in the morning or right before you go to sleep can build up unnecessary anxiety, get you into premature panic mode, put your body and mind into emergency or crisis mode, and, as a result, get your day kicked off or wrapped up the wrong way.

Taking action: This week, start your day gradually with technology and end your day unwinding yourself from it. Do not read e-mails, text messages, or listen to voice mails right after you wake up or right before you go to sleep. Allow yourself at least thirty minutes, preferably one hour after you wake up and the same before going to bed, to settle yourself.

As you progress throughout the week, record the time you spent with technology and without it.

Bryan Brooks

Day	Date	Awake Time	Sleep Time	Technology Time		Tech-Free Time	
				Hours	Minutes	Hours	Minutes
		16 Hours	8 Hours				
		16 Hours	8 Hours				
		16 Hours	8 Hours				
		16 Hours	8 Hours				
		16 Hours	8 Hours				
		16 Hours	8 Hours				
		16 Hours	8 Hours				
Totals		112 Hours	56 Hours				

Transforming Activities

Activity ideas: Go for a walk or run, go to the gym, ride your bike. Make candy or caramel apples, play a game of Horseshoes, learn about the history of your town, create a cookbook. Go go-kart racing, build a ramp for a person in a wheelchair so it is easier for them to get in and out of their house, clean a neighbor's yard that cannot do it themselves.

Other activities:

_____

_____

Tech Sabbath Habit Plan: Week 51

This week, my tech-free day is (circle one):

Mon Tues Wed Thurs Fri Sat Sun

This week's encouraging thought: Today's preparation determines tomorrow's achievement.

This week's technology challenge: Don't turn to technology as an out or as a coping device. More times than not, turning to technology during difficult situations are the paths of least resistance. It takes no effort on our part to take steps to resolve the matter. Instead, we just check out. It acts as our security blanket in times of trouble. Setting down and stepping away from the technology takes effort and accountability. Acknowledging difficult situations, discussing them, and making a clear effort shows God and the people involved that you care, are concerned, and want to work toward resolving the situation.

Taking action: This week, when difficult situations arise, don't turn to technology as an out or as a coping device. Instead, confront the situations head-on.

As you progress throughout the week, record the time you spent with technology and without it.

Bryan Brooks

Day	Date	Awake Time	Sleep Time	Technology Time		Tech-Free Time	
				Hours	Minutes	Hours	Minutes
		16 Hours	8 Hours				
		16 Hours	8 Hours				
		16 Hours	8 Hours				
		16 Hours	8 Hours				
		16 Hours	8 Hours				
		16 Hours	8 Hours				
		16 Hours	8 Hours				
Totals		112 Hours	56 Hours				

Transforming Activities

Activity ideas: Learn to salsa dance, do crossword puzzles, build a time capsule, bike ride down the steepest hill you can find, build a raft like Tom Sawyer and float down a river, give valentines and other cards two individuals who are in the local hospital, visit a rehabilitation center, learn about patients with special needs.

Other activities:

_____

_____

Tech Sabbath Habit Plan: Week 52

This week, my tech-free day is (circle one):

Mon Tues Wed Thurs Fri Sat Sun

This week's encouraging thought: You never know what you can do until you try.

This week's technology challenge: Do less technology multitasking. One of the most popular forms of technology multitasking concerns is watching TV and surfing the Internet at the same time. Constant multitasking at some point will begin to slow you down, affect your ability to concentrate and focus, as well as limit your ability to effectively process information, and you will notice yourself making more mistakes.

Taking action: This week, don't feel pressured to have to multitask with your technology.

As you progress throughout the week, record the time you spent with technology and without it.

Bryan Brooks

Day	Date	Awake Time	Sleep Time	Technology Time		Tech-Free Time	
				Hours	Minutes	Hours	Minutes
		16 Hours	8 Hours				
		16 Hours	8 Hours				
		16 Hours	8 Hours				
		16 Hours	8 Hours				
		16 Hours	8 Hours				
		16 Hours	8 Hours				
		16 Hours	8 Hours				
Totals		112 Hours	56 Hours				

Transforming Activities

Activity ideas: Do a word find or crossword puzzle, organize a self-defense workshop, sponsor a TV blackout event, start a neighborhood watch program, hang out with friends and have a barbeque, play Frisbee, jump on a trampoline, play bocce ball, have a horseshoe game tournament, play scrabble, work outside in the yard, go camping.

Other activities:

_____

_____

Living a Technology- Enhancing Life

How we manage and control the technology in our life determines whether it is a tool that enhances it or a leash that overwhelms it.

The future of technology will continue to advance and play an important role in our daily lives. It can definitely enhance life, if properly controlled and you take a break from it frequently. No question about it. However, if it is not properly controlled, it truly can be the ultimate curse, overwhelming every aspect of life. I believe what we all desire at some level is finding that perfect technology balance—one that allows us to take a break from it and use it in an intelligent way but not be controlled by it— because when you live your life with out of control technology habits and have no boundaries, it's exhausting and destructive. As the saying goes: "Too much of anything is a bad thing."

As a result of reading this book and going through the tech Sabbath habit journey, my and my family's prayer to you would be that God (Jesus Christ) would always remain first place in your life; that you would truly understand and implement His priorities and purposes for your life, His command of rest; that technology would only be a blessing to you and never a curse; that the information you learned in this book is not just read, but that it is applied year in and year out and becomes a natural part of your new well-balanced high-tech lifestyle.

By unplugging the god of technology frequently, I am confident that you too will discover for the first time or rediscover something new in the pause—the things in life that truly matter the most.

Bibliography

Every effort has been made to give complete information for all references. If the reader desires more specific information regarding any source, he or she should contact the author via e-mail at bryan@techsabbathhabit.com.

1   Article by Justin Pierce, "Family Time Decreases With Internet Use," http://uscnews.usc.edu/digital_media/family_time_decreases_with_internet_use.html

2   American Psychological Association (APA) survey

3   Survey by NPR online, " Survey Shows Widespread Enthusiasm for High Technology" http://www.npr.org/programs/specials/poll/technology/

4   Article by Media Screen, "Report: 48% of Leisure Time is Spent Online" http://www.marketingvox.com/report-48-of-leisure-time-is-spent-online-029923/

5   US Census Bureau, http://www.census.gov/PressRelease/www/releases/archives/mismobileaneous/007871.html

6   Article by W. David Gardner (Information Week Writer), "Technology Is Taking Over Americans Lives" http://www.informationweek.com/news/internet/showArticle.jhtml?articleID=196902629

7   Article by W. David Gardner (Information Week Writer), "Technology Is Taking Over Americans Lives" http://www.informationweek.com/news/internet/showArticle.jhtml?articleID=196902629

8   Pew Internet and American Life Project, "Survey Shows Users Frustrated by Technology" http://www.itbusinessedge.com/cm/community/news/bam/blog/survey-shows-users-frustrated-by-technology/?cs=20835

9   The Economist | WASHINGTON DC, http://www.economist.com/blogs/gulliver/2008/09/35_percent_SMARTPHONE_choose_over_spouse.cfm

10 Pew Internet and American Life Project, "Networked Families" http://www.pewinternet.org/Reports/2008/Networked-Families/01-Summary-of-Findings.aspx

11 Entrepreneur.com, "Consumer Technology Stats" http://www.entrepreneur.com/encyclopedia/businessstatistics/article81968.html - Cingular

12 Nielsen Media Co, "Television & Health" http://www.csun.edu/science/health/docs/tv&health.html

13 Entrepreneur.com, (Nielsen Net Ratings) "Consumer Technology Stats" http://www.entrepreneur.com/encyclopedia/businessstatistics/article81968.html

14 Entrepreneur.com, "Consumer Technology Stats" http://www.entrepreneur.com/encyclopedia/businessstatistics/article81968.html

15 NDS DVR Report, http://www.nds.com/press_releases/NDS_DVR_Survey_030908.html

16 Kaiser Family Foundation, "Media in the Lives of 8- to 18-Year-Olds", http://www.kff.org/entmedia/mh012010pkg.cfm

17 Article in Harvard Business Review by Edward M. Hallowell, "Overloaded Circuits"

18 Wired Magazine, "Americans 'Need' Their Gadgets" http://www.wired.com/science/discoveries/news/2005/12/69896

19 Pastor Rick Warren, "Four Benefits of Putting Margin in Your Life" http://www.cfaith.com/index.php?option=com_content&view=article&id=15319:four-benefits-of-putting-margin-in-your-life&catid=125:ministry

20 Article by Diane Mapes, Lifewire "Get your BlackBerry out of our bed!" http://www.cnn.com/2008/LIVING/personal/05/12/blackberries.bed/

21 Article by Jeff Seidel, "Sleep on It – 28% of Americans Get 8 Hours of Sleep on Regular Basis" http://rismedia.com/2009-03-30/sleep-on-it-28-of-americans-get-8-hours-of-sleep-on-regular-basis/#ixzz0Ly79UkEf

22 Article by Jupiter Research, "Online Ad Spending To Reach $35.4 Billion in 2012" http://www.mediapost.com/publications/?fa=Articles.showArticle&art_aid=62553

23 Article by NPD Group, "Consumer Technology Spending Reaches Record $129B" http://www.marketingcharts.com/direct/consumer-technology-spending-reaches-record-129b-3681/

24 Article by By Ned Smith, BusinessNewsDaily.com "Distracted Workers Cost U.S. Businesses $650 Billion a Year" http://www.businessnewsdaily.com/distracted-workforce-costs-businesses-billions-0589/

25 Article by By Taylor Gandossy (CNN) "TV viewing at 'all-time high,' Nielsen says" http://articles.cnn.com/2009-02-24/entertainment/us.video.nielsen_1_nielsen-company-nielsen-spokesman-gary-holmes-watching?_s=PM:SHOWBIZ

26 Article by W. David Gardner (Information Week Writer), "Technology Is Taking Over Americans Lives" http://www.informationweek.com/news/internet/showArticle.jhtml?articleID=196902629

listen|imagine|view|experience

AUDIO BOOK DOWNLOAD INCLUDED WITH THIS BOOK!

In your hands you hold a complete digital entertainment package. In addition to the paper version, you receive a free download of the audio version of this book. Simply use the code listed below when visiting our website. Once downloaded to your computer, you can listen to the book through your computer's speakers, burn it to an audio CD or save the file to your portable music device (such as Apple's popular iPod) and listen on the go!

How to get your free audio book digital download:

1. Visit www.tatepublishing.com and click on the e|LIVE logo on the home page.
2. Enter the following coupon code:
   633c-f4d1-7344-99f7-f0ea-7543-63e3-e81c
3. Download the audio book from your e|LIVE digital locker and begin enjoying your new digital enter-tainment package today!